STUDY GUIDE AND LABORATORY MANUAL

to accompany

RESEARCH IN PSYCHOLOGY
METHODS AND DESIGN

Third Edition

C. JAMES GOODWIN
Wheeling Jesuit University

JOHN WILEY & SONS, INC.

To order books or for customer service call 1-800-CALL-WILEY (225-5945).

ISBN 0-471-14998-5

Printed in the United States of America

10 9 8 7 6 5 4 3 2 1

Printed and bound by Victor Graphics, Inc.

Contents

To the Student..v

<u>STUDY GUIDE</u>

Chapter 1. Scientific Thinking in Psychology..1

Exercise 1.1. Critical Thinking About Pseudoscience.............................9

Chapter 2. Ethics in Psychological Research...13

Exercise 2.1. Role-Playing an IRB...21

Chapter 3. Developing Ideas for Research in Psychology.....................................25

Exercise 3.1. What's Next Thinking..34

Exercise 3.2. PsycINFO Search..35

Chapter 4. Measurement, Sampling, and Data Analysis......................................38

Exercise 4.1. Statistical Analysis...48

Chapter 5. Introduction to Experimental Research..54

Exercise 5.1. Identifying Independent and Dependent Variables...........63

Exercise 5.2. Detecting Flaws in Experiments.......................................65

Chapter 6. Control Problems in Experimental Research..71

Exercise 6.1. Between or Within?...80

Chapter 7. Experimental Design I: Single Factor Designs....................................85

Exercise 7.1. Identifying Experimental Designs......................................93

Exercise 7.2. Portraying Research Results...95

Chapter 8. Experimental Design II: Factorial Designs...101

Exercise 8.1. Identifying Factorial Designs...109

Exercise 8.2. Interpreting Research with Factorial Designs.................111

Chapter 9. Correlational Research..120

Exercise 9.1. Correlations and the Nature/Nurture Issue.....................129

Exercise 9.2. Assessing the Effect of Outlyers....................................130

Chapter 10. Quasi-Experimental Designs & Applied Research...........................133

Exercise 10.1. Evaluating Quasi-Experimental Designs......................142

Chapter 11. Small N Designs...148

Exercise 11.1. Outcomes of Single-Subject Designs...........................156

Chapter 12. Descriptive Research Methods..162

Exercise 12.1. Deciding on the Best Descriptive Method.....................170

Exercise 12.2. Developing Ideas for Archival Research.......................171

LAB MANUAL

Introduction..176

Lab 1. Creating False Memories..177

Lab 2. Gender Differences in Cognitive Mapping......................................181

Lab 3. The Cola Wars: A Taste Test..187

Lab 4. Context Effects in Memory..189

Lab 5. Physical Attractiveness and Punishment...192

Lab 6. Cell Phone Use and Impression Formation......................................197

References...204

To the Student:

I hope you will find this <u>Study Guide and Lab Manual</u> useful as you work your way through the research methods course. The <u>Study Guide</u> portion of this book is designed to help you master the material in the text. Researchers have known for some time that we learn better if we are actively involved with the material we are trying to master, so my main goal in the Study Guide is to get you to interact with the material in each chapter in various ways. Coordinated with each chapter in the main text, I have included:

- A set of questions for each main section of the chapter. I would suggest that as you finish studying a particular chapter section, turn to the Study Guide and write down answers to the questions corresponding to that section. Be sure you can answer them before moving on to the next section of the chapter.

- A set of key terms. These are all the concepts that appear in **boldface** print in the text; they are found also in the text's Glossary. I've provided space for you to write down definitions for these terms or examples to illustrate their meaning.

- A set of sample test items. These include fill-in items, for which the answers are always the boldfaced key terms; matching, which asks you to pair key terms with their corresponding concepts; and multiple choice questions. Answers to all the test items are on the last page of each chapter in the Study Guide. You will find detailed feedback on the multiple choice items—information about each of the alternatives, not just the correct one.

- A set of applications exercises. These are similar to the exercises found at the end of each chapter in the main text, and they provide additional experience applying the concepts learned in the chapters. Help with these exercises, or answers to them, will also be provided.

The <u>Lab Manual</u> portion of this book includes two kinds of activities. The first provides instructions and materials for a set of six empirical studies that illustrate some of the designs in the text. Their inclusion reflects my belief that the only way to learn how to do research in psychology is to do some. Your instructor will determine which studies will be completed in the course.

The second activity in the Lab Manual uses data sets that I have created, corresponding to each of the six studies. For each study, I have provided a data set for a hypothetical research outcome. Hence, in the event that you cannot complete all of the studies during the term, you will have the opportunity to "imagine" that you have completed a study and to analyze and interpret the data.

Part I

STUDY GUIDE

Chapter 1. Scientific Thinking in Psychology

Reviewing the Main Concepts
After you finish reading and studying each main section of the chapter, answer the following questions to test your comprehension. The numbers in parentheses after each question are the page numbers in the text that will help you with the answer.

- *Why Take This Course?*
  - Why is the methods course believed to provide a "foundation" for other psychology courses? Hint: process vs. content. (3)

  - Why will a research methods course help (a) the student hoping to go to graduate school in psychology, and (b) the student planning to work right after college? (4)

- *Ways of Knowing*
  - How does a belief in UFOs illustrate Peirce's tenacity idea and the concept of belief perseverance? (5-6)

  - As a way of arriving at truth, what are the advantages and disadvantages with Peirce's method of authority? (6)

o   As a way of arriving at truth, what are the advantages and disadvantages with Peirce's a priori method? (6-7)

o   There is some truth in the saying that experience is the best teacher, but what are some the problems with this old adage? Hint: think of two social cognition biases. (7-8)

- *Attributes of Scientific Thinking in Psychology*
    o   How do research psychologists use the term determinism? (9-10)

    o   How does the modern view of objectivity differ from Peirce's view? (10-11)

    o   How does objectivity relate to replication and why was objectivity a problem for early introspective psychologists? Hint: think of the quotes in Box 1.1. (12)

    o   How does Sir Francis Galton illustrate the tendency for researchers to be data-driven? (13)

- Why isn't this an empirical question? "Are people basically good or evil?" (14)

- What are the features of scientific thinking that go into making someone a "skeptical optimist?" (14)

- *Psychological Science and Pseudoscience*
  - List the four main attributes of pseudoscientific thinking. (16-22)

  - Consider phrenology and the use of subliminal tapes. How have they been associated with legitimate science? (16, 19-20)

  - What is the problem with anecdotal data? (20-21)

  - How did phrenologists get around the problem that not all killers had bumps in their "destructiveness" area? What's wrong with this strategy? (21-22)

- In what way does the subliminal tape business illustrate the fourth and final attribute of pseudoscientific thinking (complexity reduced to simplicity)? (22)

- For legitimate scientists, phrenology was destroyed by the ablation studies completed by Flourens. Describe what he did. (17-19)

- *The Goals of Research in Psychology*
  - What are the four main goals of scientific psychology? (22-24)

- *A Passion for Research in Psychology (Part I)*
  - What does the work of Eleanor Gibson and B. F. Skinner have in common? (25-28)

Key Terms
Each of the following terms will be (a) printed in boldface in the chapter, and (b) found in the glossary at the end of the text. After you finish reading and studying the chapter, try to write definitions of each or examples that illustrate each. In parentheses after each term I've put the page on which it first appears.

Tenacity (5)

Belief perseverance (6)

Authority (6)

A priori method (7)

Empiricism (7)

Availability heuristic (7)

Confirmation bias (7)

Determinism (9)

Discoverability (9)

Statistical determinism (9)

Objectivity (10)

Introspection (11)

Data driven (11)

Empirical question (14)

Pseudoscience (15)

Anecdotal evidence (20)

Effort justification (21)

Description (23)

Laws (23)

Prediction (23)

Explanation (23)

Control (24)

Sample Test Items

<u>Fill-ins</u>

The answers to these fill-in-the-blank questions can be found in the list of key terms.

1. John strongly believes that people on welfare are not interested in working; his tendency to pay special attention when stories about welfare fraud appear on TV is an example of the social cognition bias called _____.

2. Phred the phrenologist believes the area of "Destructiveness" was located just above the top of the ears and pointed out that many vicious killers had enlargements in that part of their skull . The type of evidence being used by Phred is called _____ evidence.

3. TV commercials trying to persuade you to buy a product because 9 out of 10 doctors recommend it are asking you to rely on Peirce's method of _____.

4. As psychologists use the term, _____ simply means that behaviors occur in certain situations regularly enough to be predicted with some degree of certainty greater than pure chance.

5. Ed says he has a headache. His verbal description of how it feels is an example of a(n) _____ report. Because only he can experience it, his description lacks _____.

6. Psychological scientists try to ask _____ questions, that is, question answerable with data.

7. Sarah, who watches a lot of shows featuring real police chasing criminals, believes she is highly likely to be a victim of a carjacking. Her belief reflects the social cognition bias of the _____.

8. When psychological scientists use the word _____ to describe one of the goals of psychology, they are referring to the application of psychological principles to improve the human condition.

9. Ann is showing indications of _____ when she says that the $50 subliminal tape she has been using has been remarkable in its ability to make her stop smoking.

10. On the basis of careful observations, a researcher classified children's play into three categories: solitary, parallel, and interacting. This work is a good example of the research psychologist's goal of _____.

Matching

Terms in the left-hand column are key terms. For each term, find the correct matching example or concept description or example, and write in the letter of the term in the blank space.

A. belief perseverance   _____   enables predictions to be made

B. availability heuristic   _____   Galton and the effectiveness of prayer

C. objectivity   _____   overestimating based on vivid memory

D. empiricism   _____   an explanation for everything

E. data driven   _____   observable to more than one person

F. anecdotal evidence   _____   only recalls events consistent with one's opinion

G. law   _____   "I know it's true. End of discussion."

H. authority   _____   experience is the best teacher

I. pseudoscience   _____   questionable due to effort justification

J. confirmation bias   _____   "I don't know. What does the book say?"

Multiple Choice

1. What is the most important way in which a research methods course differs from a course in social psychology?
    a. the methods course will have a focus on ethics, while the social psychology course will not consider ethics
    b. the social psychology course will have a greater emphasis on statistics
    c. the methods course will emphasize how research occurs, while the social psychology course will focus on the research outcomes themselves
    d. the social psychology course will emphasize process, while the research methods course will emphasize content

2. Which of the following is true about belief perseverance?
    a. it is the basis for Peirce's way of knowing called the "a priori" method
    b. it is a tendency for events to stand out in our minds because we keep seeing them on the news
    c. it refers to the fact that most of our strong beliefs are formed in childhood, and last throughout adulthood
    d. it refers to an unwillingness to have one's opinions changed, even by solid scientific evidence

3. To illustrate the weakness of _____ as a way of knowing, Peirce pointed out that philosophers have been debating different sides of the mind-body question for hundreds of years.
    a. tenacity
    b. the a priori method
    c. the method of authority
    d. empiricism

4. Ed believes he is in telepathic communication with Sally because it seems like every time he thinks of her, she calls him on the phone. He ignores all the times he is thinking of her and she doesn't call. That is, he is being affected by
    a. a confirmation bias
    b. the availability heuristic
    c. statistical determinism
    d. belief perseverance

5. One of the main reasons why behaviorism became popular in the United States was that
    a. it relied on introspection as a means of understanding why we do things
    b. its way of defining what was being studied met the scientific criterion of objectivity
    c. it emphasized research, while introspective psychologists were not interested in research
    d. it took complex concepts and reduced them to simplistic ideas that were easily understood

6. Of the following questions, only one is an empirical question. Which one?
    a. Can people be truly evil?
    b. Are people basically good, but corrupted by society?
    c. Will males or females be more likely to give blood?
    d. How does the mind exert its influence of the physical body?

7. How do psychological scientists use the concept of determinism?
    a. they believe that human behavior can be predicted with more than chance probability
    b. they believe that it means free choice is impossible
    c. they believe that our behaviors have been predetermined from our births
    d. they don't use it – they reject it

8. What does it mean to say that advocates of a pseudoscience "sidestep disproof?"
    a. they divorce themselves completely from legitimate science, calling scientists "those of little faith"
    b. apparent disproof can be explained away by proposing additional mechanisms to account for the problem
    c. they only mention supporting evidence; nonsupporting evidence is forgotten
    d. they use definitions of terms that are so precise that when apparent disproof occurs, they just say the result must refer to some other phenomenon

9. After research shows that a form of behavior therapy can reduce phobic responses, therapists begin using the technique in their practices. Which of the goals of research in psychology is being reflected here?
    a. explanation
    b. prediction
    c. description
    d. control

10. When explaining behavior, psychologists are generally willing to say that factor X is causing phenomenon Y to occur when several criteria have been met. Which of the following is not one of those criteria?
    a. other explanations for Y can be ruled out
    b. X comes before Y
    c. in terms of some theory, X "makes sense" as an explanation for Y
    d. Y always occurs when X is present

Applications Exercise

1.1. Critical Thinking About Pseudoscience

One of the features of Chapter 1 is a discussion of pseudoscience and how it compares to legitimate science. This exercise involves searching the internet for a website that promotes some pseudoscientific theory or a product based on pseudoscience. The theory or product should relate to psychology in some fashion. Your goal is to do a critical analysis of the claims made on the website, using the criteria described in the chapter for identifying pseudoscience. Turn in answers to the following questions; also print out the first page of the website.
As a starting point to find lots of good examples of bad science, check out these websites:
    1. the website for the magazine "The Skeptical Inquirer" – www.csicop.org
    2. a website that reprints articles debunking pseudoscience, but also includes links to some pseudoscientific websites – www.pseudoscience.org

1. Write down the address (URL) of the pseudoscience website you have located.

2. Describe the primary claim being made by the website. That is, is it attempting to sell a product by arguing that it will improve your life somehow? Is it advocating some technique or therapy that will change your behavior?

3. Does the website attempt to associate itself with more legitimate science? In what manner does this occur?

4. Can you give examples of how the site uses anecdotal data to support its claims.

5. Is there any indication in the website of pseudoscience's tendency to sidestep disproof? Describe.

6. Is there any indication of pseudoscience's tendency to reduce complex concepts or phenomena to overly simplistic concepts? Describe.

7. Is there anything else about the website that arouses your scientific skepticism? Describe.

8. Who is the author of the website? What are the author's credentials?

Answers to Sample Test Items

<u>Fill-ins</u>

1. confirmation bias
2. anecdotal
3. authority
4. statistical determinism
5. introspective; objectivity
6. empirical
7. availability heuristic
8. control
9. effort justification
10. description

<u>Matching</u>

From top to bottom, the correct letter sequence is: G, E, B, I, C, J, A, D, F, H

<u>Multiple Choice</u>

1. a. ethics will be a part of both courses
   b. the opposite is true
   c. CORRECT ANSWER – this reflects the process/content distinction
   d. the opposite is true

2. a. the "a priori" method concerns the use of logic and persuasive argument
   b. this is the availability heuristic
   c. overstates the importance of childhood
   d. CORRECT ANSWER

3. a. has problems as a way of knowing, but not this one
   b. CORRECT ANSWER – a priori method being Peirce's label for a reliance on logical argument
   c. problematic because authorities can be wrong
   d. not used by Peirce

4. a. CORRECT ANSWER
   b. tendency to think that events which stand out in memory occur more often than they really do
   c. belief that events can be known with greater than chance accuracy
   d. belief held strongly, even in the face of contradictory evidence

5. a. behaviorists rejected introspection
   b. CORRECT ANSWER – behaviors can be measured objectively (i.e., two observers can agree that a particular behavior occurred)
   c. introspective psychologists were very interested in research
   d. this is an attribute of pseudoscience; introspective psychologists were legitimate scientists

6. a. not easily answerable with data
   b. not easily answerable with data
   c. CORRECT ANSWER
   d. not easily answerable with data

7. a. CORRECT ANSWER
    b. unless events are to some degree predictable, useful choices cannot be made
    c. this is a form of "predestination" – psychologist reject this
    d. may be true of some humanistic psychologists, but not true of the majority of psychologists

8. a. they actually try to associate themselves with real science
    b. CORRECT ANSWER – for instance, when confronted with a murderer with a small area of destructiveness, phrenologists would show how the person could be "explained" by some other combination of faculties
    c. true enough about pseudoscience, but not the "sidesteps disproof" problem
    d. their definitions of terms are very imprecise

9. a. explanation would concern why the therapy worked
    b. prediction would refer to the lawful relationship between the therapy and its outcome
    c. description would provide a clear narrative account of the therapy
    d. CORRECT ANSWER – control, as a goal of experimental psychology, does not mean coercion, but application

10. a. an important criterion
    b. also an important criterion
    c. this one too
    d. CORRECT ANSWER – it is more accurate to say that Y occurs when X is present "with a greater than chance probability"

Feedback on Applications Exercises

There are no "correct" answers here, but if you would like some help with doing a critical analysis of a website, check out this site:

http://lib.nmsu.edu/instruction/eval.html

Chapter 2. Ethics in Psychological Research

Reviewing the Main Concepts

After you finish reading and studying each main section of the chapter, answer the following questions to test your comprehension. The numbers in parentheses after each question are the page numbers in the text that will help you with the answer.

- *Developing the APA Code of Ethics*
    - o The work of the Hobbs committee in developing APA's first ethics code is a good illustration of Chapter's 1's description of research psychologists as "data-driven." Explain. (37)

    - o The most recent code has 6 general principles. Can you describe any three of them? (37)

    - o The code distinguishes between general principles and specific standards. Distinguish between principles and standards. Hint: think of the terms "aspirational" and "enforceable." (37-38)

    - o With regard to ethics, how did John Watson justify completing the Little Albert study? (36)

- *Ethical Guidelines for Research with Humans*
    - o Before undertaking any research project in psychology, researchers must deal with a fundamental dilemma. What is it? (39)

o   What is the role of an IRB and who is on a typical IRB? (41)

o   What determines whether and IRB will undertake an expedited or a formal review? (41)

o   Why are some psychologists critical of IRBs? (41)

o   How does an IRB decide between studies involving "minimal risk" and studies in which participants will be "at risk?" (42)

o   If you collect some data as an experimenter in this research methods course, who is responsible for assuring that the study is conducted according to the APA code of ethics? (42)

o   How do research psychologists use the term informed consent? What are the elements that are included in any informed consent form for use with adult research participants? (43-44, 49-50)

o How do research psychologists justify the use of deception in research? Use Milgram's study as an example. (39,44-46)

o How does consent with adults different from consent when children are used as participants? (49-50)

o How did those completing the Willowbrook and Tuskegee studies justify their research and how was their rationale different from the one used for MK-ULTRA? (47-49)

o What is involved in a typical debriefing session? (53)

- *Ethical Guidelines for Research with Animals*
  o Those arguing against the use of animals in research vary in terms of the strength of their arguments. How do moderately opposed advocates differ from those absolutely opposed? (55)

  o In his defense of the use of animals in research in psychology, Miller makes three points. What are they? (57-58)

- What does the ethics code for animals have in common with the code for humans? What is the most obvious difference? (59-60)

- What does the code say about the use of animals for educational purposes? (60)

- The APA developed guidelines for the use of animals before they developed an ethics code for human research. What were the elements of the first animal code? (57)

- *Scientific Fraud*
  - How does research fraud differ from carelessness and what are the two main varieties of fraud in psychological research? (60-61)

  - It is generally believed that when researchers falsify data, they will be discovered in one of three ways? What are they? (61-62)

  - Assuming for the moment that the Burt case illustrates data falsification, what does the case point out about the difficulty of detecting fraud? (62-63)

Key Terms

Each of the following terms will be (a) printed in boldface in the chapter, and (b) found in the glossary at the end of the text. After you finish reading and studying the chapter, try to write definitions of each or examples that illustrate each. In parentheses after each term I've put the page on which it first appears.

Ethics (34)

Critical incidents (37)

Research participants (39)

Subject (39)

Institutional Review Board (IRB) (41)

Informed consent (44)

Deception (44)

Assent (49)

Debriefing (53)

Dehoaxing (53)

Desensitizing (53)

Plagiarism (61)

Falsifying data (61)

Sample Test Items

Fill-ins

The answers to these fill-in-the-blank questions can be found in the list of key terms.

1. A debriefing that adequately alleviates the participant's stress but fails to make the true purpose of the study clear has succeeded at _____ but failed at _____.

2. The first APA ethics code was developed empirically using the _____ procedure.

3. Potential research participants who receive enough information to make a reasonable decision about whether to volunteer for a study have satisfied that ethical requirement for

   _____.

4. _____ is a type of scientific fraud that involves deliberately using the ideas of someone else without giving proper credit to the source.

5. Individuals who volunteer to participate in research have been referred to historically as _____, but today the term is seldom used, except when referring to animals in research.

Matching

Terms in the left-hand column are key terms. For each term, find the correct matching example or concept description or example, and write in the letter of the term in the blank space.

A. ethics   _____   sufficient information to decide to participate

B. IRB   _____   only in a study involving deception

C. informed consent   _____   stealing an idea

D. data falsification   _____   principles for behaving as a good person

E. dehoaxing   _____   method for developing first ethics code

F. desensitizing   _____   often detected through failure to replicate

G. plagiarism   _____   post experiment requirement

H. critical incidents   _____   judges ethical adequacy of a study

I. debriefing   _____   reducing stress of a participant

1. Which of the following is true about Watson and Rayner's Little Albert study?
    a. they had parental consent but lacked Albert's assent
    b. they were able to justify doing it because they removed the fear at the end of the study
    c. its main purpose was to try out various ways of removing a fear in a child who was afraid of rabbits
    d. they did not think that an unusual level of harm would occur because similar fears would be learned by Albert anyway

2. The requirement for informed consent in research with human participants
    a. is one of the six "general principles" of the 1992 code
    b. means that deception about the true purpose of a study is not allowed in research with humans
    c. is not needed unless the participants are "at risk"
    d. means that sufficient information must be available for people to decide whether to participate

3. Consider the following hypothetical titles of articles from journals in psychology. Which of them is most likely to have required a formal review by an IRB?
    a. the effects of crowding on depression
    b. gender differences in the content of personal ads
    c. the influence of repeated practice on recall from long-term memory
    d. a survey of attitudes toward animal research

4. Which of the following statements would you be *least likely* to find in an informed consent form?
    a. there is no penalty for not starting the study, but once you begin, you are obligated to complete the session
    b. your data will be coded in a way that will protect your identity
    c. the full purpose of the study will be explained to you at the end of the session and the complete results of the study will be available to you when the study is over
    d. this study has been approved by the university's Institutional Review Board (IRB)

5. As used in Chapter 2, the term "desensitizing" refers to
    a. exposing participants to repeated deception (they get used to it)
    b. the part of debriefing designed to alleviate any stress experienced by the participant
    c. the reassuring effects on participants when they have the opportunity to read and sign a consent form
    d. explaining the true purposes and hypotheses of the study once a session has been completed

6. From an ethical standpoint, what was the most serious problem with Milgram's study?
    a. there was no debriefing
    b. there was no attempt to follow up on people to see if they had been adversely affected by the experience
    c. participants who wished to stop were told they had to continue
    d. by using a captive population (college students required to participate) he failed to meet the need for informed consent

7. Consider the Willowbrook, Tuskegee, and MK-ULTRA projects. What did they all have in common?
    a. they all had the ultimate goal of improving medical practice
    b. by using children, they all failed to gain assent, even though they did gain consent
    c. they all failed to meet the criterion of informed consent
    d. all three studies were rejected by IRBs, yet were conducted anyway

8. In a study of concept learning in first-graders, all of the following should happen except
    a. to help make the experience enjoyable, children should be given substantial incentives to participate
    b. parents must give consent
    c. teachers of the children in their classes should give consent
    d. the children should be asked if they are willing to participate

9. The goal of MK-ULTRA was to
    a. see if LSD could have beneficial medical effects
    b. determine whether LSD could be used as an effective weapon in the Cold War
    c. conduct basic research on the psychological effects of a new and unknown drug – LSD
    d. see if taking LSD would improve Army morale

10. Neal Miller's article on the use of animals in psychological research is described in Chapter 2. According to Miller,
    a. using animals is OK for medical research, but animals shouldn't be used to study psychology
    b. psychology could not progress without studying animals, especially when you consider that about half of all research in psychology uses animals
    c. animal research should be limited to primates because they are more similar to humans than other animals
    d. studying animal behavior not only benefits humans, animals benefit as well

11. All of the following are part of the ethics code for animal research except
    a. the researcher must be an expert concerning the species being studied
    b. procedures using reinforcement are preferred over those using punishment
    c. animal studies that are purely educational in purpose cannot be done
    d. if the animal must be killed at the end of the study, a painless procedure must be used

12. The Burt case illustrates the fact that
    a. falsified data might not be noticed if other research produces the same conclusions
    b. scientific fraud is often caught when odd results fail to replicate
    c. quite a bit gets missed in the peer review process for journals
    d. it is usually easy to spot falsified data – they just seem too bizarre to the experienced scientist

Applications Exercise

2.1. Role-Playing an IRB

Read each of the following descriptions of research carefully and consider the ethical issues involved. After each description, identify and describe any potential ethical problems that would need to be resolved before the study could be approved by an IRB. In particular, keep these questions in mind:

- What is the level of risk to participants and what specific risks exist in the study?
- Is the value of the study sufficient to offset any potential risk to participants?
- What safeguards must be in place to protect the participants?
- Is there anything in particular that ought to be stressed in the consent form?
- Would some individuals be unsuitable as participants in the study?

1. A researcher is interested in what makes some people persevere more than others. She develops a procedure in which participants will be asked to solve a series of 10 anagrams (scrambled letters that have to be rearranged to form a word). Participants are given 20 seconds to solve each anagram. Then at the end of 20 seconds, they are asked if they want another 20 seconds, and strongly encouraged to keep going. This continues until the anagram is solved or the participant gives up (i.e., no longer perseveres). To examine the effects of "social comparison" on performance, some participants are told that most students usually solve all 10 problems, but that some of the anagrams are harder than others. Others are told nothing about how typical students perform. Participants are tested individually. What they don't know is that anagrams #3, #5, and #9 have NO solution – they are unsolvable. These of course are the anagrams of interest to the researcher, who wants to know how soon people will give up trying to solve them.

Your analysis:

2. A researcher wishes to see if feelings of reduced competence will make people more willing to volunteer for some task they might ordinarily avoid. He designs a study in which participants are led to believe they will be trying to identify concepts. They are shown several sets of slides and for each set, they are asked to write down what the items on the slides have in common. After doing this ten times, participants are told the results. In particular, they are told that most college students average about 6-7 correct, but they only had 2 correct answers. Participants in a second group (perceived competence not reduced) are told they had 8 correct. All participants are tested individually. On the way out of the lab, participants are approached by another student, apparently unconnected with the concept identification experiment, and asked if they would be willing to give blood. The experiment ends after the participant responds to the request (i.e., no actual blood drawn). The researcher hypothesizes that reduced-competence participants will be more likely to volunteer, in order to give their self-esteem a boost.

Your analysis:

3. A researcher believes that if people are feeling moderately anxious, their anxiety can be heightened by adding a sense of being crowding. She designs a study in which participants sign up for a study on the effects of anxiety on memory. They are informed that shock will be present in the study. One group is told that when they make a mistake on the memory test, they will receive a small shock ("it will feel like your skin is buzzing"). A second group is told that the shocks will not be severe but they will be moderately painful (but won't cause permanent tissue damage). Half of the participants in each group are asked to wait for the study to begin in a waiting room that is no bigger than a closet. Remaining participants are not crowded – they wait in a much larger waiting room. After spending 10 minutes in the waiting rooms, participants are asked to fill out an "anxiety" survey, and their blood pressure and pulse are recorded. No memory experiment occurs and no shock is administered. The researcher expects the maximum anxiety to be felt by those expecting moderate shock and waiting in the closet-sized room.

Your analysis:

4. A researcher believes that undeclared students whose parents have divorced within the past five years will take longer to decide on a major and will show higher levels of depression and anxiety than (a) undeclared students whose parents are not divorced and (b) undeclared students whose parents divorced more than five years ago. He sends a survey to all of the university's seniors who were known (Registrar's records) to have begun their college careers without having declared a major. The survey (a) asks them to indicate when they declared a major, (b) includes a series of items designed to measure their current levels of depression and anxiety, and (c) asks a series of questions about their parents' marital status and the relationship between the student and his or her parents.

Your analysis:

Answers to Sample Test Items

Fill-ins

1. desensitizing, dehoaxing
2. critical incidents
3. informed consent
4. plagiarism
5. subject

Matching

From top to bottom, the correct letter sequence is: C, E, G, A, H, D, I, B, F

Multiple Choice

1. a. it is not clear that consent was given; Albert was too young for assent to be possible
   b. they failed to remove the fear
   c. this was the purpose of the Mary Cover Jones study
   d. CORRECT ANSWER – this was their pragmatic rationale for doing the study; they also
      believed Albert was physically strong and would be able to withstand the procedures

2. a. it is a "standard" not a "general principle"
   b. deception is allowed under certain circumstances
   c. consent is needed except under very limited circumstances (e.g., naturalistic observation)
   d. CORRECT ANSWER – note that the requirement is not that participants know every single
      detail about the study, however

3. a. CORRECT ANSWER – crowding could be traumatic and depression is a clinical term;
      participants would probably be at risk in this study
   b. participants not involved
   c. minimal risk – expedited review OK
   d. minimal risk – expedited review OK

4. a. CORRECT ANSWER – participants must be allowed to discontinue participation
   b. confidentiality
   c. debriefing
   d. important provision

5. a. doing this would be unethical
   b. CORRECT ANSWER
   c. not relevant
   d. this is "dehoaxing"

6. a. debriefing occurred – its extent is unclear
   b. Milgram used a psychiatrist to check on participants' reactions
   c. CORRECT ANSWER – this conflicts with the principle that uncomfortable participants
      should be given the opportunity to quit the experiment without penalty
   d. by recruiting in the local community, he specifically avoided using college students

7. a. true only of the first two
   b. only the Willowbrook study used children
   c. CORRECT ANSWER – what little consent existed in these studies was far from informed
   d. IRBs didn't exist when these studies began

8. a. CORRECT ANSWER – substantial incentives can be coercive
   b. this should happen
   c. so should this
   d. so should this (assent)

9. a. some research had this goal, but not the MK-ULTRA project
   b. CORRECT ANSWER – its effects were not well known at the time
   c. the military tends to fund applied rather than basic research
   d. not relevant

10. a. using animals is OK for both medical and psychological research
    b. less than 10% of research in psychology uses animals
    c. Miller didn't argue this, nor would other advocates of animal research
    d. CORRECT ANSWER – for example, improving zoos

11. a. important part of the code
    b. also important
    c. CORRECT ANSWER – under certain circumstances, animals can be used for purely educational purposes
    d. also important

12. a. CORRECT ANSWER – like other researchers, Burt presented data supporting the importance of a genetic factor in intelligence
    b. Burt produced results that later replicated
    c. true, but not relevant in the Burt case
    d. often true, but not relevant in the Burt case

Feedback on Applications Exercise

There are no absolutely correct answers to these IRB proposals. They provide food for thought and give you a chance to think apply how to apply the code in real research situations. Nonetheless, here are some potential risks to consider for each of the four situations.

1. Especially for participants in the condition in which they think other students are solving the impossible anagrams, but to some degree for all participants, there will be a fair amount of stress and frustration experienced when they encounter the key anagrams. The consent form should perhaps make a special point about reminding participants that that they stop the experiment at any time, and debriefing will be important as well.

2. This is a problem similar to number one, in that participants are being made to feel stress, in this case a lowering of their sense of competence. The IRB might also consider whether another volunteer activity (other than giving blood) might accomplish the same goals. In general, the IRB will have to look closely at the relative value of the research, compared to the level of deception involved.

3. The informed consent procedure will have to be clear about the shock levels to be expected (even though no participant actually receives any shock) and of course the debriefing must be thorough. The researcher also should consider some pre-screening of participants. Those with any degree of claustrophobia should probably be screened out.

4. The main problem here is maintaining the anonymity of participants. The IRB will be looking for specifics about how the researcher will maintain confidentiality and, if the survey is to be done by mail, how some form of debriefing will occur. Also, the researcher might be asked to provide a means for follow-up and care in the event the survey creates a high level of stress, especially for those students of recently divorced parents.

Chapter 3. Developing Ideas for Research in Psychology

Reviewing the Main Concepts
After you finish reading and studying each main section of the chapter, answer the following questions to test your comprehension. The numbers in parentheses after each question are the page numbers in the text that will help you with the answer.

- *Varieties of Psychological Research*
  - Give an example from the area of human memory that illustrates the distinction between basic and applied research. (70)

  - Where do the Milgram obedience studies stand with reference to the distinction between (a) basic and applied research, (b) laboratory and field research, and (c) mundane and experimental realism? (70, 72-73)

  - Consider the Dutton and Aron studies on romantic love and show how they combine the best features of field and laboratory research. (73-75)

  - What are the ethical implications of the decision about whether to conduct research in the field or in a lab? (76)

  - Distinguish quantitative from qualitative research. (75-77)

- *Asking Empirical Questions*
    - o Using hunger as an example, explain why psychologists try to use operational definitions. (77-78)

    - o Three different studies of aggression might use three different operational definitions of aggression. Research psychologists don't necessarily see this as a weakness. Why? (78)

- *Developing Research from Observations and Serendipity*
    - o What were the origins of the research that led to the so-called Zeigarnick effect? (79)

    - o Describe two example of research that illustrate the phenomenon of serendipity. (80-82)

- *Developing Research from Theory*
    - o What are the four defining features of any theory? (82)

    - o Use learned helplessness theory to demonstrate the meaning of the term "construct." (83-84) o   With an answer that incorporates the terms deduction and induction, describe the circular relationship between theory and data. (84)

o   Research outcomes either support or fail to support theories. Why do research psychologists avoid saying that outcomes prove or disprove theories? (85-86)

o   Why is it important for theories to be capable of falsification? Use phrenology as an example. (87-88)

o   Why is it important for explanations to be parsimonious? Use Clever Hans as an example. (88-90)

- *Developing Research from Other Research*
    o   What is meant by the "what's next?" question and why is this question so important in understanding the development of research projects? (92)

    o   What is a pilot study and what is its purpose? (92)

- A fair amount of research could be characterized as involving replication and extension. Explain. (93-94)

- *Creative Thinking in Science*
  - How does the creation of maze learning as a method illustrate Pasteur's point about chance favoring the "prepared mind?" (94-96)

- *Reviewing the Literature*
  - What is PsycINFO? (97)

  - Describe any three tips for expediting a literature search with PsycINFO. (97-99)

Key Terms

Each of the following terms will be (a) printed in boldface in the chapter, and (b) found in the glossary at the end of the text. After you finish reading and studying the chapter, try to write definitions of each or examples that illustrate each. In parentheses after each term I've put the page on which it first appears.

Basic research (70)

Applied research (70)

Laboratory research (72)

Field research (73)

Mundane realism (73)

Experimental realism (73)

Quantitative research (75)

Qualitative research (75)

Operationism (77)

Operational definitions (77)

Converging operations (78)

Serendipity (80)

Theory (82)

Construct (84)

Deduction (84)

Hypothesis (84)

Induction (84)

Productivity (87)

Falsification (87)

Parsimonious (88)

Programs of research (91)

Research team (92)

Pilot study (92)

Replication (93)

Extension (93)

Partial replication (93)

Creative thinking (94)

Sample Test Items

<u>Fill-ins</u>

The answers to these fill-in-the-blank questions can be found in the list of key terms.

1. According to Aronson, it is generally true that an experiment with _____ realism has more value to science than a study with _____ realism.

2. Near the end of Chapter 1, you learned how Skinner produced his first extinction curves when the food magazine broke; this event illustrates the phenomenon of _____.

3. Hypotheses are derived from theory through the logical process of _____.

4. A dog's escape behavior could be the result of trial-and-error learning or it could be an example of sophisticated reasoning and planning by the dog. The first explanation is more _____ than the second.

5. A researcher is trying to design a study to rule out the possibility that a rat needs its sense of smell to learn a maze. This is an example of what Popper called a _____ strategy.

6. The theory of cognitive dissonance, proposed in the 1950s, is still leading to predictions that result in research. That is, on the criterion of _____ the theory has been a very good one.

7. A general category of research that de-emphasizes the importance of statistical analysis is known as _____ research.

8. _____ thinking occurs in science when a researcher sees a connection between two seemingly unrelated ideas.

9. Jack has developed an elaborate procedure for a study on cognitive mapping. Before starting the experiment, he collects data on a few people to determine if his procedure is

appropriate and understandable to participants. That is, Jack has conducted a

_____.

10. A good _____ will describe a construct in terms of a specific and easily measurable behavior.

Matching

Terms in the left-hand column are key terms. For each term, find the correct matching example or concept description or example, and write in the letter of the term in the blank space.

A. basic research   _____ to show that Clever Hans couldn't do math

B. applied research   _____ Milgram's study had plenty of it

C. induction   _____ adequate explanation with fewest assumptions

D. experimental realism   _____ more likely to occur in than out of the lab

E. falsification   _____ summarizes existing knowledge

F. replication   _____ inferred from behavior

G. hypothesis   _____ Egeland's research on reading

H. theory   _____ from specific findings to broad conclusions

I. construct   _____ increases confidence in the validity of a study

J. parsimonious   _____ educated guess about a study's outcome

Multiple Choice

1. Statistical analyses are least likely to be found in
    a. applied research
    b. qualitative research
    c. field research
    d. basic research

2. Which of the following is true about field research?
    a. it can involve applied research, but it is more likely to involve basic research
    b. unlike laboratory research, ethics is seldom a problem in applied research
    c. it can produce results that improve the lives of those being studied
    d. because of the lack of control, field research is always qualitative research

3. For drawing conclusions about human behavior, Aronson argued that experimental realism was more critical than mundane realism. What does it mean to say that a study is high in experimental realism?
    a. it is a tightly controlled experiment, occurring in a laboratory setting
    b. it involves basic research (the distinction reflects Aronson's preference for basic over applied research)
    c. it means that even if the study takes place in a lab, to the participants it seems like an everyday real-life situation
    d. it means that participants become involved in the study and behave naturally

4. Which of the following is true about the Dutton and Aron studies on romantic love?
    a. good example of how a finding is strengthened if it happens both in the lab and in the field
    b. good illustration of the strengths of qualitative research
    c. its shortcomings are a good example of the need for parsimonious explanations
    d. high on mundane realism; low on experimental realism

5. What is meant by the concept of "converging operations?"
    a. it refers to studies using different operational definitions that yield similar results
    b. it refers to the combined results of several studies using identical operational definitions
    c. over the years, consensus emerges in different labs about the one true operational definition of a construct
    d. it refers to the process by which ideas for applied research derive from the findings of basic research

6. Chapter 1's description of how Skinner first produced an extinction curve is a good example of
    a. a parsimonious explanation
    b. falsification as a strategy
    c. a serendipitous finding
    d. scientific creativity

7. On the basis of some theory, a prediction about the outcome of an experiment is made. The experiment does not come out as expected. What is most likely to be concluded?
    a. the theory has been disproven and should be discarded
    b. the experiment does not support the theory
    c. the experiment was not done properly
    d. the experiment tells us nothing about the theory

8. All of the following are true about theories except
    a. they organize and summarize existing knowledge about a topic
    b. they are tentative until the facts prove them true
    c. they provide possible explanations for the phenomenon under study
    d. they lead to testable hypotheses through the process of deduction

9. Young boys imitate their fathers at times. According to the text, the learning theory explanation for this phenomenon has an edge over the Freudian theory because
    a. learning theory has been productive, but Freud's theory has generated very little research
    b. learning theory has been shown to be true, whereas Freudian theory has been falsified
    c. learning theory is more parsimonious than Freudian theory
    d. none of the above – because of its greater complexity, Freudian theory can explain much more than learning theory

10. Pfungst demonstrated that when Clever Hans's questioner did not know the answer to a math problem, Hans didn't know it either. This demonstration is an example of
   a. falsification
   b. productivity
   c. parsimony
   d. serendipity

11. According to the text, the most common source of ideas for new research in psychology is
   a. some everyday observation that generates curiosity
   b. unanswered questions from a study recently completed
   c. deduction from theory
   d. serendipity

12. Which of the following is true about the relationship between theory building and data collection?
   a. when studies come out as expected, inductive support for the theory is gained
   b. if an experiment fails, discarding the experiment is an example of affirming the consequent
   c. when a hypothesis is not supported, virtually nothing has been learned about the theory
   d. a good theory will be inclusive enough to explain every possible research outcome

Applications Exercises

3.1. What's Next Thinking

What follows is a description of one of social psychology's most famous experiments, ranking right up there with Milgram's obedience studies. Read it carefully, and then place yourself in the role of a researcher planning the next study. That is, given the results of the study as described, what variations in procedure might you make in order to learn more about the phenomenon in question? Think of it as a two-step process. First, think of a possible explanation for the results. Second, think of some variation in procedure that could assess your explanation. For example, one possible explanation for the outcome of the Milgram obedience study was that the authority figure was perceived as an expert (after all, the study was done at Yale and they ought to know what they are doing, right?). To evaluate this explanation, a next study could change the perception of the authority figure, perhaps by running the study in a non-university location. Milgram in fact did this and the obedience levels indeed declined.

The Asch conformity study.

In the 1950s Solomon Asch completed a series of studies showing that under the right circumstances, people were remarkably willing to conform to the opinions and judgments of others. They were even willing to deny the evidence of their own eyes if that evidence was in conflict with a group decision. In the basic conformity study, Asch's method was as follows:

The study appeared to be a perception problem in which participants examined a card with three vertical lines on it. The lines varied in length. The task was to look at a second card with a single vertical line and judge which of the three lines on the first card matched it in length. It was an extremely easy task – the three lines on the first card varied by quite a bit and when people were tested one at a time, they hardly ever made any errors (<1%). Asch tested male college students in groups of 6-8, but only one of the persons was a true participant. The others appeared to be students but were actually part of the experiment (usually referred to as experimental "confederates"). The real participant was seated in the next to last position around a table. On a given trial, one person at a time would make his judgment, with the real participant being the next to last to make his choice. On certain trials, the confederates were cued to deliberately choose the wrong line (and all confederates chose the same wrong line). Faced with the evidence of their own eyes and the conflicting responses of a unanimous group, participants went along with the group and gave what they must have known to be the wrong response about 37% of the time, a huge difference in performance compared to when students were tested without a group present.

What could be a reason for this conforming behavior?

How might you vary the procedure to see if your proposed reason has could indeed influence conformity?

3.2. PsycINFO Search

This exercise requires that you have access to PsycINFO. If your school gets PsycINFO via CD-ROM, the database will be on CD-ROM drives and limited to the number of copies your school has bought. If your school uses PsycINFO online, the database is probably available from any networked computer on campus and can be accessed through such systems as EBSCOhost. However you gain access to it, practice some of the search tips in Chapter 3 of the textbook, and then complete the following exercise:

1. Find and print out the full listing (i.e., including the Abstract) for the Egeland (1975) study that is in Chapter 3. The full reference to the study can be found in the textbook's Reference section.

2. Identify 4 different research topics that Egeland has investigated in his career. Find and print out the full listing for one study in each topic.

3. Find and print out the full listing (i.e., including the Abstract) for the Dutton and Aron (1974) study that is in Chapter 3. The full reference to the study can be found in the textbook's Reference section.

4. Find and print out the full listings for any follow-up or similar studies on the same topics by the same authors.

5. Determine what other research topics have interested both Dutton and Aron over the years. Find and print out two studies for each person, each dealing with a topic unrelated to romantic love.

Answers to Sample Test Items

Fill-ins

    1. experimental; mundane
    2. serendipity
    3. deduction
    4. parsimonious
    5. falsification
    6. productivity
    7. qualitative
    8. creative
    9. pilot study
    10. operational definition

Matching

    From top to bottom, the correct letter sequence is: E, D, J, A, H, I, B, C, F, G

Multiple Choice

1. a. both basic and applied research are highly likely to include statistical analyses
    b. CORRECT ANSWER – there might be some summary statistics in a qualitative study, but for the most part, the results will be reported as a narrative analysis
    c. field research, unless it is qualitative research, will be likely to use statistical analysis
    d. both basic and applied research are highly likely to include statistical analyses

2. a. the opposite is true
    b. ethical issues occur in all psychological research
    c. CORRECT ANSWER – the Sternberg research on cognitive functioning of children infected with intestinal parasites is a good example
    d. field research can easily be quantitative

3. a. non-lab studies can easily have experimental realism
    b. applied research can easily have experimental realism
    c. whether it seems like real-life is not relevant to the issue of experimental realism
    d. CORRECT ANSWER – it's best if participants are involved in the procedure

4. a. CORRECT ANSWER – the lab study controlled for "type of men in the study" and strengthened the overall conclusion about romantic love
    b. it is not an example of qualitative research
    c. Dutton and Aron's explanations for the outcome are reasonably parsimonious
    d. in the lab study, high on mundane; in the field study, high on both

5. a. CORRECT ANSWER – studies using different operational definitions of hunger in a maze study was the example used in the chapter
    b. different researchers often use different operational definitions
    c. might be true, but not what is meant by converging operations
    d. not relevant

6. a. not relevant
    b. not relevant
    c. CORRECT ANSWER – he returned to find the effects of a jammed pellet dispenser
    d. what he did after making the serendipitous discovery might have been creative

7. a. one disconfirming experiment won't eliminate a theory
   b. CORRECT ANSWER – notice that the theory isn't discarded just on the basis of one disconfirmation
   c. worth checking out, but not necessarily the problem
   d. the experiment might raise questions about the theory if it was run properly

8. a. part of the standard definition
   b. CORRECT ANSWER – this is the common misconception about theory
   c. part of the standard definition
   d. part of the standard definition

9. a. both theories have been productive
   b. close, but this greatly overstates the case
   c. CORRECT ANSWER – fewer assumptions in learning theory
   d. Freudian theory's complexity and vagueness has led to charges that it is not testable

10. a. CORRECT ANSWER – the higher mental ability (math skill) was ruled out (falsified)
    b. not relevant
    c. parsimony comes into play when Pfungst proposed an simpler explanation for the horse's apparent skill
    d. not relevant

11. a. important source of ideas, probably a close second
    b. CORRECT ANSWER – the result of an answer to the "what's next?" question
    c. close, and somewhat related to alternative b.
    d. also important, but not as common as the other three alternatives

12. a. CORRECT ANSWER – note that there is no mention of the theory being "proven"
    b. affirming the consequent occurs when the experiment succeeds, and the researcher erroneously concludes that the theory has been shown to be true
    c. non-support can say a lot about a theory (e.g., lead to modifications)
    d. not good – if this happens, the theory cannot be falsified and is therefore useless

Feedback on Applications Exercises

1. Here are some possible variations on the Asch study, but I'm sure you can think of more.
        - make the perceptual task more difficult – conformity should increase
        - have one of the confederates break with the majority – conformity should decrease

2. PsycINFO search. You should not have difficulty finding these articles.

Chapter 4. Measurement, Sampling, and Data Analysis

Reviewing the Main Concepts
After you finish reading and studying each main section of the chapter, answer the following questions to test your comprehension. The numbers in parentheses after each question are the page numbers in the text that will help you with the answer.

- *What to Measure – Varieties of Behavior*
  - What are two different ways in which researchers develop measures for constructs? (107)

  - The "gravity" study is a good example of how operational definitions can be used to bring seemingly unmeasurable constructs into the lab. Explain. (108-109)

  - Describe how reaction time can be used to measure visual imagery. (110)

  - Historically, how was the reaction time method first used? (111-112)

- *Evaluating Measures*
  - How can you tell when a measure is reliable? (112-113)

- What is the difference between the face validity and the criterion validity of a measure of behavior? (114)

- Use Mischel's "delay of gratification" research to illustrate what is meant by construct validity. (114-115)

- Measures can be reliable without being valid, but if a measure is valid, you can assume that it is also reliable. Explain (hint: phrenology example). (115-116)

- *Scales of Measurement*
    - Give an example to show that you understand nominal scales of measurement. (116-117)

    - Give an example to show that you understand ordinal scales of measurement. (117-118)

    - What is the difference between an interval and a ratio scale of measurement? (118-120)

- *Who to Measure - Sampling*
  - o What is the goal of probability sampling? (121)

  - o What is self-selection and why is it a problem in surveying? (121-122)

  - o Distinguish between a simple random sample and a stratified sample. (122-124)

  - o What is cluster sampling and when is it used? (124-125)

  - o What is convenience sampling and why is it so popular among research psychologists? (125)

- *Statistical Analysis*
  - o Distinguish between descriptive and inferential statistics. (127)

  - o Distinguish between the mean, median, and mode. (127-128) o   When is it better to use a median rather than the mean? (128)

o   When reporting a set of scores, why is it important to report not just the mean, but also the standard deviation, or some other measure of variability? (128-129)

o   What is a stem and leaf display and what does it show? (132-133)

o   When creating a graph, why is it important to be careful about the labeling of the Y-axis? (134-135)

o   Describe how testing the null hypothesis is similar to testing the guilt of someone in a courtroom. (136-137)

o   Describe what is meant by the phrase "rejecting the null hypothesis." (137)

o   What is a Type I error? Give an example. (138-139)

o   What is a Type II error? Give an example. (138-139)

o   What is power and what factors influence it? (140)

o   What question is answered by an effect size analysis? (140-141)

Key Terms
Each of the following terms will be (a) printed in boldface in the chapter, and (b) found in the glossary at the end of the text. After you finish reading and studying the chapter, try to write definitions of each or examples that illustrate each. In parentheses after each term I've put the page on which it first appears.

Reliable (112)

Measurement error (112)

Valid (114)

Face validity (114)

Criterion validity (114)

Construct validity (114)

Measurement scale (116)

Nominal scale (116)

Ordinal scale (117)

Interval scale (118)

Ratio scale (120)

Population (121)

Sample (121)

Representative sample (121)

Biased sample (121)

Self-selection (122)

Simple random sample (122)

Stratified sample (124)

Cluster sample (124)

Convenience sample (125)

Descriptive statistics (127)

Inferential statistics (127)

Mean (127)

Median (128)

Median location (128)

Mode (128)

Range (129)

Standard deviation (129)

Variance (129)

Histogram (129)

Frequency distribution (129)

Normal curve (132)

Stem and leaf display (132)

Null hypothesis (136)

Alternative hypothesis (137)

Alpha (a) level (137)

Type I error (138)

Type II error (138)

Systematic variance (139)

Error variance (139)

Power (140)

Effect size (140)

Sample Test Items

<u>Fill-ins</u>

The answers to these fill-in-the-blank questions can be found in the list of key terms.

1. If there is a great deal of _____, then reliability will be low.

2. If scores on some measure (e.g., an IQ test) are good at predicting future performance (e.g., grades in school), the measure will be said to have _____ validity.

3. Scores on most personality tests are measured on a(n) _____ scale.

4. The goal of random sampling is to select a sample that is _____ of the population as a whole.

5. Most research in psychology uses a _____ sample.

6. In general, _____ statistics are used when answering the question, "How would you best summarize the performance of participants on the color blindness test?"

7. If a single number is used to describe a set of scores, and you know that an equal number of scores occurred above and below the reported number, you know that the number is the _____.

8. The most frequently used measure of the variability in a set of scores is the _____.

9. A researcher finds a significant difference in map-reading skill between males and females. Several other labs attempt to replicate the finding and all fail to get the same results. If this failure to replicate continues, suspicion will grow that the initial study was a _____ error.

10. In a typical inferential analysis, the researcher hopes that _____ variance will be high, and _____ variance will be low.

Matching

Terms in the left-hand column are key terms. For each term, find the correct matching example or concept description or example, and write in the letter of the term in the blank space.

A. range	_____ somatotypes
B. measurement error	_____ directly related to sample size
C. interval scale	_____ classifying events
D. biased sample	_____ score seen most often
E. null hypothesis	_____ predicting the 1936 President
F. nominal scale	_____ high score minus low score
G. Type II error	_____ fail to find a true difference
H. power	_____ nonprobability sampling
I. mode	_____ no true difference
J. convenience sample	_____ reduces reliability

1. Which of the following was true about the Kim and Spelke study on the development of the concept of gravity?
   - a. it relied on the use of reaction time methodology
   - b. after habituation occurred, it was assumed that if the child understood gravity, it would pay the most attention to an event that was consistent with the law of gravity
   - c. after habituation occurred, it was assumed that if the child understood gravity, it would pay the most attention to an event that violated the law of gravity
   - d. after habituation occurred, it was assumed that if the child understood gravity, it would pay the most attention to an event that had two stimulus changes rather than one

2. In the Shepard and Metzler study on mental rotation, it was assumed that
   - a. males would outperform females on the task
   - b. decision times would be proportional to the amount of mental rotation required to make the stimuli overlap
   - c. reaction time would be faster for pairs rotated 180° than for pairs rotated 90°
   - d. the task was actually a verbal one—they were trying to falsify the idea that visual imagery could be involved

3. If a measure used in psychology is reliable, then
   - a. it will have zero measurement error
   - b. it will probably also be valid
   - c. it can be used to predict what someone will do
   - d. taking a second measurement will produce a similar result

4. Phrenologists believed that the faculty of "amativeness," or physical love, was located in the area of the cerebellum. They would measure the width of the head just below and behind the ears. We now know that the cerebellum controls motor coordination. Which of the following is true?
   - a. the phrenologists' measure was probably very reliable
   - b. the phrenologists' measure was both reliable and valid
   - c. the phrenologists' measure was neither reliable nor valid
   - d. the phrenologists' measure must have contained a great deal of measurement error

5. Which of the following empirical questions is most likely to be answered by a measure using a nominal scale of measurement?
   - a. Are psychology majors or biology majors more likely to be Democrats?
   - b. When ranking movies for levels of sex and aggression, do males and females differ?
   - c. Will rats make more errors in a maze when they are hungry or when they are full?
   - d. Will endomorphs tend to be viscerotonic or cerebrotonic?

6. What differentiates interval from ratio scales of measurement?
   - a. interval scales have equal intervals between points on the scale – ratio scales don't always have these equal intervals
   - b. in ratio scales, a higher number always means "more" of the phenomenon being measured; interval scales don't maintain this "order" characteristic
   - c. scores of zero are not possible on interval scales
   - d. on ratio scales, a score of zero means the absence of the phenomenon being measured

7. Consider the following pairs of measures and measurement scales. Which one of them is inappropriately paired?
   a. temperature in Celsius – ratio
   b. scores on a 7-point scale of somatotonia – interval
   c. class standing (first in the class, second, etc.) – ordinal
   d. gender – nominal

8. Suppose you wish to test a representative sample of people in your theology class on attitudes toward the idea of women as priests. There are 40 people in the class, 30 females and 10 males. What would be the best strategy?
   a. simple random sample
   b. cluster sample
   c. stratified sample
   d. convenience sample

9. When probability sampling is called for, but the complete list of people in the population is missing, which procedure will be used?
   a. simple random sampling
   b. cluster sampling
   c. stratified sampling
   d. convenience sampling

10. Suppose you learn that the IQs of the six professors in your psychology department are as follows: 89, 154, 93, 83, 90, and 79. If someone asks, "What's the overall level of intelligence in the department?" what should you calculate?
    a. the median
    b. the mode
    c. the mean
    d. the range

11. There is an example in the chapter of a golf pro with two classes, one at 8:00 and one at 9:00. For the 8:00 group, the typical 9-hole scores were 50, 52, 58, 46, and 54. For the 9:00 group, these scores were 36, 62, 50, 72, 40. What was the point of the example?
    a. it showed that when describing data, you should report both the mean and the median
    b. it showed that when describing data, you should report both the mean and the standard deviation
    c. it showed that inferential statistics are more crucial than descriptive statistics
    d. it showed that Type I errors are more important than Type II errors

12. Suppose you want to display the results of a survey on student shyness visually. Assume that shyness scores range from 10 to 200. What should you do?
    a. create a simple frequency distribution
    b. group the data and create a grouped histogram (e.g., one bar for those scoring between 10 and 30)
    c. construct a normal curve of the data
    d. build a stem and leaf display

13. In a study examining gender differences in "sense of direction," which outcome would be a Type I error?
    a. in the population, males are better, but your study failed to find a gender difference
    b. in the population, no real difference occurs, but the males in your study performed significantly ($p<.05$) worse than the females
    c. you fail to reject the null hypothesis, but you should have done so
    d. you reject the null hypothesis, when in fact a true difference exists

Applications Exercise

4.1. Statistical Analysis

Imagine that you are in a theories of personality class with 41 other students; in all, there are 21 males and 21 females. The instructor hands out a personality test that measures shyness on an interval scale, with scores ranging from 5 (not very shy, indeed very outgoing) to 50 (extremely shy). Here are the scores for the students in your class:

Males				Females		
23	36	19		26	33	43
45	39	42		19	20	32
40	37	26		17	24	26
20	34	42		35	28	22
30	29	35		30	33	27
46	41	32		29	18	26
30	36	28		34	31	37

1. For the class as a whole, calculate the mean, the median, the range, the variance, and the standard deviation. Create a stem and leaf display.

2. For the males in the class, calculate the mean, the median, the range, the variance, and the standard deviation. Create a stem and leaf display for the males.

3. For the females in the class, calculate the mean, the median, the range, the variance, and the standard deviation. Create a stem and leaf display for the females.

4. To compare the shyness scores for males and females, use the guidelines in Appendix C of the main text to complete a t test for independent groups and to calculate the effect size. What can be concluded about the shyness levels of the males and females in your theories of personality class?

Answers to Sample Test Items

Fill-ins

    1. measurement error
    2. criterion
    3. interval
    4. representative
    5. convenience
    6. descriptive
    7. median
    8. standard deviation
    9. Type I
    10. systematic; error

Matching

    From top to bottom, the correct letter sequence is: C, H, F, I, D, A, G, J, E, B

Multiple Choice

1. a. it relied on habituation methodology
    b. an event consitent with gravity would result in continued habituation in this case
    c. CORRECT ANSWER - an event violaing gravity would catch this child's attention
    d. this was in fact true for the child who did not grasp gravity (the 5 month olds)

2. a. this is indeed an outcome of this research, but not an *assumption* at the outset
    b. CORRECT ANSWER – this was their rationale for using reaction time
    c. the opposite would be expected
    d. their research supported the idea that visual imagery existed

3. a. all measures have some degree of measurement error – none is perfect
    b. not necessarily – see the next question
    c. this is only true is the measure is also valid
    d. CORRECT ANSWER – this is a common way to asses reliability

4. a. CORRECT ANSWER – their measures would be the same tomorrow as today
    b. they were reliable but not valid
    c. they were reliable
    d. because they were reliable, the opposite was true

5. a. CORRECT ANSWER – categories are involved here
    b. the term "ranking" is a tip-off that an ordinal sclae is involved
    c. errors – true zero possible, therefore ratio
    d. interval scales in Sheldon's body type research

6. a. both interval and ratio scales maintain the equal interval assumption
    b. "order" is maintained in both interval and ratio scales
    c. scores of zero can occur on interval scales, but they aren't a true zero
    d. CORRECT ANSWER – this is a true zero

7. a. CORRECT ANSWER - $0°$ is not a true zero (i.e., the absence of temperature) – this is an interval scale
    b. equal interval but no zero
    c. class standing = class rank
    d. two categories

8. a. not a good idea with such a disproportion of males and females and an issue on which makes and females might be expected to differ
    b. no need – the sample frame is small and known
    c. CORRECT ANSWER – it will be important for the male-female proportion in the sample to match the proportion in the class
    d. this situation calls for a probability sample (i.e., clearly representative)

9. a. to do simple random sampling, you need a complete list of people
    b. CORRECT ANSWER – you will sample from clusters of people defined in some way
    c. stratified sampling also requires a complete list of people
    d. convenience sampling is not an example of probability sampling procedure

10. a. CORRECT ANSWER – the extreme score would produce a mean that distorted the true picture
    b. no score is repeated, so the mode is not relevant
    c. not with the extreme score
    d. the question calls for a measure of central tendency, but the range is a measure of variability

11. a. not relevant here
    b. CORRECT ANSWER – the means are the same for both groups, but there is much more variability in the second group
    c. both descriptive and inferential statistics are important
    d. both types of errors are important

12. a. the range of scores is so big the distribution would not look good
    b. this could work, but unlike the stem and leaf display, the grouped histogram would not allow you to identify the actual scores
    c. the normal curve is a theoretical curve – you want a picture of actual (empirical) data
    d. CORRECT ANSWER – the display is good when there is a wide range of scores and it still enables you to identify each score precisely

13. a. this is a concrete example of a Type II error
    b. CORRECT ANSWER – you think there is a difference, but there really isn't
    c. this is a more abstract description of a Type II error
    d. this isn't an error at all – in fact, it is the ideal outcome

Feedback on Applications Exercise

1. For the group as a whole:

Mean shyness score	=	30.95
Median shyness score	=	30.50
Range	=	29.00
Variance	=	60.22
Standard deviation	=	7.76

Stem and leaf display:

Stem	Leaves
0	
1	7 8 9 9
2	0 0 2 3 4 6 6 6 6 7 8 8 9 9
3	0 0 0 1 2 2 3 3 4 4 5 5 6 6 7 7 9
4	0 1 2 2 3 5 6

2. For the males:

Mean shyness score	=	33.81
Median shyness score	=	35.00
Range	=	27.00
Variance	=	61.15
Standard deviation	=	7.82

Stem and leaf display:

Stem	Leaves
0	
1	9
2	0 3 6 8 9
3	0 0 2 4 5 6 6 7 9
4	0 1 2 2 5 6

3. For the females:

Mean shyness score	=	28.10
Median shyness score	=	28.00
Range	=	26.00
Variance	=	45.02
Standard deviation	=	6.71

Stem and leaf display:

Stem	Leaves
0	
1	7 8 9
2	0 2 4 6 6 6 7 8 9
3	0 1 2 3 3 4 5 7
4	3

4. Results of t test and effect size analysis:

$t(40) = 2.54$, $p = .015$

$d = .55$

Males are shyer than females in this class, the difference is significant, and the effect is a medium-sized one.

Chapter 5. Introduction to Experimental Research

Reviewing the Main Concepts
After you finish reading and studying each main section of the chapter, answer the following questions to test your comprehension. The numbers in parentheses after each question are the page numbers in the text that will help you with the answer.

- *Essential Features of Experimental Research*
    o What was Woodworth's basic distinction (in his "Columbia bible") between experimental and correlational research? (148-149)

    o What are the three essential features of any experiment in psychology? (149)

    o What is an independent variable and what is meant by the term "levels" of an independent variable? (149)

    o Give examples of independent variables that are (a) situational, (b) task, and (c) instructional in nature. (150)

    o Distinguish between an experimental and a control group. (150-151)

- o What is a confounding variable and why is it a problem in experimental research? (151-152)

- o Using the construct of anxiety, show how it could be an independent variable, a dependent variable, or an extraneous variable in need of being controlled. (153)

- • *Manipulated versus Subject Variables*
  - o What is meant by a subject variable? Give two examples. (153-155)

  - o When drawing conclusions from studies using manipulated variables, statements about cause can be made. These statements cannot be made when using subject variables. Why? (155-156)

  - o In the famous Bobo study, identify the primary manipulated independent variable and its levels, the subject variable, the dependent variables, and one of the controls employed to avoid confounding. (157-158)

- • *The Validity of Experimental Research*
  - o Give two examples of mistakes that result in a loss of statistical conclusion validity. (159)

- Use a study of the effects of TV violence on children's aggression to illustrate the meaning of construct validity, as it applies to experiments. (159-160)

- What is the "college sophomore" problem and how does it relate to an experiment's validity? (160-161)

- How does the distinction between individualist and collectivist cultures relate to an experiment's validity? (163)

- Using memory research as an example, explain what is meant by ecological validity. (163)

- In general, what characterizes an experiment said to be high on internal validity? (164-165)

- *Threats to Internal Validity*
  - Using the example of a program designed during the first semester of college to reduce test anxiety, explain how the internal validity of a study could be reduced by either history or maturation. (166)

o   Give an example of regression to the mean. How can it affect a study's internal validity? (166-168)

o   Distinguish between testing and instrumentation as threats to the internal validity of a study. (168)

o   The presence of a pretest, by itself, can influence the outcome of a study. Describe how pretest effects can be evaluated by means of a design created by Solomon. (168-169)

o   What is a subject selection effect and how did it affect the validity of the "ulcers in executive monkeys" study? (169-171)

o   How might attrition reduce an experiment's internal validity? In what sense can an attrition effect be seen as similar to a subject selection effect? (171-172)

Key Terms

Each of the following terms will be (a) printed in boldface in the chapter, and (b) found in the glossary at the end of the text. After you finish reading and studying the chapter, try to write definitions of each or examples that illustrate each. In parentheses after each term I've put the page on which it first appears.

Experiment (149)

Independent variable (149)

Field experiment (149)

Field research (149)

Situational variable (150)

Task variable (150)

Instructional variable (150)

Experimental group (150)

Control group (150)

Extraneous variable (151)

Confound (151)

Dependent variable (152)

Subject variable (153)

Statistical conclusion validity (159)

Construct validity (160)

External validity (160)

Ecological validity (163)

Internal validity (164)

Pretest (165)

Posttest (165)

History (166)

Maturation (166)

Regression to the mean (166)

Testing (168)

Instrumentation (168)

Subject selection (169)

Attrition (171)

Sample Test Items

<u>Fill-ins</u>

The answers to these fill-in-the-blank questions can be found in the list of key terms.

1. One of the defining features of any experiment is the careful attempt to control _____ variables

2. Age, gender, and socioeconomic class are all examples of _____ variables.

3. Concern over _____ validity has led memory researchers to investigate such things as the reasons why we forget our keys and our ability to recognize people from old high school yearbooks.

4. A manipulated independent variable is called a(n) _____ variable when the two groups in the study are told to use different rehearsal strategies when memorizing a list of words.

5. Although he normally shoots in the high 80s or low 90s for 18 holes, Jim manages to shoot a 78. Because he knows about the phenomenon of _____, he won't be surprised if his next round is in the mid-80s.

6. _____ is a threat to internal validity that comes about because the effects of some significant event occurring between pretest and posttest.

7. The _____ validity of a study will be low if the study includes a confounding factor.

8. The _____ validity of a study will be called into question if the researcher completes a *t* test when a different type of test should have been chosen.

Matching

Terms in the left-hand column are key terms. For each term, find the correct matching example or concept description or example, and write in the letter of the term in the blank space.

A. maturation   _____ a behavior being measured

B. external validity   _____ type of manipulated independent variable

C. attrition   _____ participants don't return for the posttest

D. dependent variable   _____ developmental changes from pre- to posttest

E. subject selection effect   _____ when extraneous variable is left uncontrolled

F. subject variable   _____ already-existing attribute of participant

G. instrumentation   _____ participants in two groups not equal at outset

H. confound   _____ measuring tool changes from pre- to posttest

I. task variable   _____ experimental treatment withheld

J. control group   _____ generalizes to other situations

Multiple Choice

1. In an experiment studying the effect of X_1 and X_2 on Y,
   a. there will be two dependent variables
   b. X_1 is an independent variable and X_2 is an extraneous variable that needs to be controlled
   c. Y will be some measure of behavior
   d. not enough information to tell which is the IV and which is the DV

2. Which of the following is true about Woodworth's so-called "Columbia bible?"
    a. it was the first to distinguish between subject and manipulated independent variables
    b. it created the scales of measurement (nominal, ordinal, interval, ratio)
    c. it made a clear distinction between experimental and correlational research
    d. it was the first to distinguish between internal and external validity

3. All experiments in psychology will include
    a. attempts to control extraneous variables
    b. at least one subject variable
    c. a control group
    d. at least two dependent variables

4. In a study about the ways in which anxiety can influence people's ability to solve problems efficiently, an experimenter identifies two groups of people – some are characteristically anxious while others are more relaxed types of people. Both groups are given several problems to solve. Which of the following is true?
    a. anxiety in this case is a situational variable
    b. problem solving is a manipulated independent variable
    c. the description of the outcome will not be likely to mention the term "cause"
    d. because they are told to solve problems, the independent variable here is an instructional variable

5. In a study designed to improve adherence to an exercise program, a researcher compares males and females who either (a) enter a program that rewards them concretely for attending sessions, (b) enter a program that tries to make them feel guilty for not attending sessions, or (c) enter a control group that does not have a specific program. Which of the following is true?
    a. there are three different groups of participants in this study
    b. the study includes both a manipulated variable and a subject variable
    c. there are two dependent variables in the study
    d. both variables being tested are subject variables

6. When a confounding factor exists in an experiment,
    a. it has more of an effect in external validity than internal validity
    b. it means there will be at least two different explanations for the results of the study
    c. it means a subject variable has been used instead of a manipulated variable
    d. it means the experimenter has failed to include a control group

7. Research in psychology is sometimes criticized because the findings are based on studies using participants from a single cultural group. This is a criticism of
    a. statistical conclusion validity
    b. ecological validity
    c. external validity
    d. internal validity

8. In a study of the effects of frustration on aggression, a researcher uses questionable operational definitions of both terms. What effect will this have on the validity of the study?
    a. it will raise questions about construct validity
    b. it will reduce the external validity of a study, but not affect construct validity
    c. it will inevitably introduce a confound into the study
    d. it won't affect validity, but the reliability of the measures will be low

9. A program is developed to help males cope with stress. Between the pretest and posttest all the males retire. Stress is lower on the posttest than on the pretest. The program might have reduced stress, but another likely explanation is possible. Which of the following "threats" to internal validity provide the most likely alternative explanation?
     a. instrumentation
     b. regression
     c. maturation
     d. history

10. Which of the following is true about research participant pools?
     a. since the 1992 revision of the APA ethics code, they are no longer allowed
     b. students should be aware of their existence when they sign up for the course
     c. if the research participation takes 20 minutes, the alternative activity, for those who don't want to be participants, must also take exactly 20 minutes
     d. students don't need to be told about alternatives to participation unless they ask about them specifically

11. In a program designed to improve self-esteem, the researcher worries that the items on the pretest might sensitize participants to the goals of the program and this pretest knowledge by itself might influence the outcome. This threat to internal validity is called
     a. testing
     b. instrumentation
     c. history
     d. a selection effect

12. In Joseph Brady's famous study on "executive" monkeys, which of the following was true?
     a. the monkeys kept dying, so attrition made it impossible to draw firm conclusions
     b. by putting easily-conditioned monkeys in the executive group, he introduced a subject selection confound
     c. by the end of the study, stress levels were reduced in the executive monkeys, but the result was probably a regression effect
     d. he compared two different types of monkeys (a subject variable) when he should have attempted a manipulated variable

Applications Exercises

5.1. Identifying Independent and Dependent Variables

For each of the following descriptions of studies, (a) identify the independent variable(s) and their levels, (b) indicate whether these variables are manipulated or subject variables, (c) indicate whether the manipulated variables are situational, task, or instructional variables, and (d) identify and name the measurement scale for the dependent variable(s).

1. In a study of the effects of REM-sleep deprivation, volunteers spend 3, 4, or 5 nights in a sleep lab. While in the lab, they are placed in one of three different groups. One group is awakened every time they enter REM-sleep (as you recall from general psychology, REM-sleep is a time when dreaming occurs). A second group is awakened during non-REM-sleep, and a third group is allowed to sleep through the night. After the experience, the participants are tested on reaction time, a set of anagram problems (each problem involves taking a set of scrambled letters and rearranging them into a word), and a self-report survey in which they indicate (on a series of 1-5 scales) the extent to which the experience has affected them.

2. In a cross-cultural study of helping behavior, a researcher sets up a helping situation in which male or female adolescents ask male or female adults (natives in the country being studied) for directions to a train station. The study is completed in the New York, Paris, Rome, and London.

3. In a study of crowding, introverts and extraverts are recruited and placed into two groups. Some are tested in a large room (8' x 8'), others in a medium-sized room (6' x 6') and still others are tested in a small room (4' x 4'). To see if expectations will influence the outcome, half the participants in each room are told that the study is hypothesizing that crowding will harm their performance; the remaining participants are told nothing about the hypothesis. While in the room, participants fill out an anxiety survey (psychological test), then listen to a series of brief segments of five heavy metal songs and rank them from the most annoying to the least annoying.

4. In a study of the effects of cognitive processing on distance estimation, participants are blindfolded and led by the experimenter along a one of two pre-planned routes inside the psychology building (one straight; one with several turns). During the trip, some participants listen to a tape and attempt to shadow it (i.e., as they hear the words, they must repeat them out loud); others listen to the tape with the expectation that they will have to recall information about it later. Others have no cognitive activity. At the end of the trip, participants estimate the distance (in feet) they have just walked and indicate (on a 10-point scale) how confident they are about their distance estimate.

5. In a study of first impressions, college students see a brief video of a college-aged person being interviewed. For half the participants, the interview is described as a job interview (i.e., the person being interviewed might be get a job); the remaining participants are told the interview is a clinical interview (i.e., the person being interviewed might be admitted to a psychiatric hospital). Also, half the participants in each condition are told to concentrate on what is being said in the interview and half are told to concentrate on the person's physical mannerisms. After seeing the video, participants indicate whether or not they would like the person to be their roommate and rate the person on a series of ten different personality scales.

5.2. Detecting Flaws in Experiments

Each of the following hypothetical experiments has at least two methodological flaws (confounds). Identify them and indicate how they could be corrected in order to make the studies methodologically sound.

1. As part of a class research project, a group of three student-researchers (Ed, Ted, and Fred) decide to study the effects of physical attractiveness on ratings of success. Participants look at a set of five photos of highly attractive people, then five more photos of moderately attractive people. Finally, they see photos of five unattractive people. Previous research identified appropriate photos for each condition. To get a good cross-section of students, the researchers decide to test three types of students: psychology majors, business majors, and chemistry majors. By a random process, it is determined that the psychology majors will be tested by Ed, that Ted will test the business majors, and that Fred will test the chem majors.

2. A hospital administrator wants to make the birthing process less stressful for mothers. A study is set up in which expectant mothers are given the opportunity to volunteer for a program in which they give birth in a hospital room that is set up more like a real bedroom than an operating room. Twenty mothers volunteer. To compare the experience with a more traditional birthing procedure, the administrator randomly selects twenty other women, who undergo a more traditional operating room procedure. Because the procedure is experimental and could be risky, only doctors with at least fifteen years of experience are assigned to the new birthing room. Level of experience is not considered to be an important factor in the traditional environment.

3. In a cognitive mapping study, a researcher wants to determine if geographic orientation will help students identify the locations of buildings on campus. A map of the campus is prepared that includes only the border of the school and the location of the psychology building (the experiment takes place in this building). In order, participants are asked to mark on the map the locations of four buildings: the chapel, the gym, the dining hall, and a men's' dorm. After participants identify the locations of the chapel and the gym, the experimenter indicates the location of north on the map, to see if giving this geographic orientation will improve the accuracy for the final two locations.

4. An educational researcher believes that the use of a study guide will improve grades and hopes to find evidence to support that belief. The researcher teaches two sections of a course in educational psychology and after flipping a coin, decides to make the study guide a required purchase in the 8:00 section but not required for the 2:00 section. To be sure that students are using the study guide properly, the researcher has them turn in weekly assignments based on study guide activities. Students in the "control group" aren't given homework assignments.

Answers to Sample Test Items

Fill-ins

   1. extraneous
   2. subject
   3. ecological
   4. instructional
   5. regression to the mean
   6. history
   7. internal
   8. statistical conclusion

Matching

   From top to bottom, the correct letter sequence is: D, I, C, A, H, F, E, G, J, B

Multiple Choice

1. a. X_1 and X_2 are independent variables, not dependent variables
   b. the "effect of X on Y" formulation says nothing about extraneous variables
   c. CORRECT ANSWER - Y is the dependent variable
   d. there is plenty of information

2. a. it didn't mention the distinction, and most of its contents involved what we would today call manipulated independent variables
   b. this actually happened at about the same time (1930s) but Woodworth didn't do it
   c. CORRECT ANSWER – and he implied that correlational had second-class status
   d. this happened much later

3. a. CORRECT ANSWER – confounding is problem to be avoided in all experiments
   b. subject variables may or may not be present
   c. all experiments have controls, but not necessarily a control group
   d. many studies (if not most) have just a single dependent variable

4. a. anxiety is a subject variable in this example
   b. problem solving is the dependent variable
   c. CORRECT ANSWER – because a subject variable is involved the researcher will be cautious in drawing conclusions, saying only that the two groups performed differently
   d. an instructional variable exists when different groups are given different instructions

5. a. there are three different groups of males and three groups of females – six groups in all
   b. CORRECT ANSWER – program type is manipulated; gender is a subject variable
   c. there is no information about dependent variables mentioned
   d. only gender is a subject variable in the study

6. a. the opposite is true
   b. CORRECT ANSWER – the outcome could be due to the IV, the confound, or some combination of the two
   c. whether a subject or a manipulated variable has been used has, by itself, no relevance for confounding
   d. confounding is indeed a failure to control some extraneous factor, but it is possible to maintain control without necessarily including a control group

7. a. this has to do with whether that statistical analyses were chosen and completed properly
   b. this is a form external validity, but it refers to whether the results are relevant for those situations that involve everyday living
   c. CORRECT ANSWER – the criticism concerns whether the results generalize to "other populations"
   d. this concerns whether there has been a failure to control extraneous variables

8. a. CORRECT ANSWER - it will be difficult to learn anything about frustration and aggression from this study
   b. this study probably will lack external validity, but it will also fail the construct validity criterion
   c. even with bad operational definitions of terms, it still could be confound-free
   d. there's nothing in the question that enables one to conclude anything about reliability

9. a. there's no reason to assume that the measures will change between pre- and posttesting
   b. there is no indication of extreme scores on the pretest, although it's possible that the only people who signed up were highly stressed
   c. it's unlikely that maturational changes will occur in 6 months for adults
   d. CORRECT ANSWER – retirement is a big event that might reduce stress by itself

10. a. they are no allowed, but must follow specific guidelines
    b. CORRECT ANSWER – notification should be made part of the course registration process
    c. the alternative activity should provide an equivalent experience, but doesn't have to match participation minute for minute
    d. they must be told of alternatives to participation right from the start, in order to make an informed choice

11. a. CORRECT ANSWER – the Solomon design could be used to evaluate pretest effects
    b. this is a problem when the measuring instrument itself changes in some manner from pretest to posttest, so that the tests aren't equivalent
    c. there doesn't seem to be a relevant event occurring between pretest and posttest
    d. no indication that subject selection will produce nonequivalent groups here (in fact, it looks like there is just a single group)

12. a. all the monkeys died who started the study ended it as well
    b. CORRECT ANSWER - the easily-conditioned happened to be more ulcer-prone
    c. stress levels were quite high in the executive monkeys, as evidenced by their ulcers
    d. actually, his study amounted to one using a subject variable (level of emotionality in the two groups), but he intended a manipulated variable

Feedback on Applications Exercises

Identifying Independent and Dependent Variables

1. IV#1: number of nights in the lab (three levels: 3, 4, or 5 nights)
             manipulated; situational
   IV#2: sleep condition (three levels: REM-deprived; non-REM-deprived; control)
             manipulated; situational
   DVs: reaction time (ratio); anagram solving (ratio); survey (interval)

2. IV#1: country studied (four levels: US, France, Germany, Italy)
   subject
   IV#2: gender of those asking for help (two levels: male, female)
   Manipulated (participants have an equal chance of being asked by either a male or female adolescent); situational
   IV#3: gender of those being asked for help (two levels: male, female)
   subject
   DV: whether or not participants give directions (nominal)

3. IV#1: personality type (two levels: introvert, extravert)
   subject
   IV#2: room size (three levels: large, medium, small)
   manipulated; situational
   IV#3: outcome expectation (two levels: crowding mentioned; crowding not mentioned)
   manipulated; situational
   DVs: anxiety survey (interval); song rankings (ordinal)

4. IV#1: shape of route (two levels: straight, with turns)
   manipulated; situational
   IV#2: cognitive activity (three levels: shadow, listen, none)
   manipulated; task
   DVs: distance estimation (ratio); confidence (interval)

5. IV#1: expectation of interview (two levels: job interview, psychiatric interview)
   manipulated; situational
   IV#2: participant focus (two levels: on verbal, on mannerisms)
   manipulated; instructional
   DVs: whether or not to be a roommate (nominal); personality ratings (interval)

Detecting Flaws in Experiments

1. Confound #1. sequence: every participant sees the photos in the same order; seeing the attractive people first might produce an effect different from seeing the unattractive ones first; to correct the problem, randomize the order of presenting the photos.

   Confound #2. experimenter: each of the experimenters might run the session in slightly different ways; thus if there is a difference in ratings between psychology and business majors, it could be due to something about the ways Ed and Ted ran the sessions (maybe their biases affected the way they gave the instructions); to correct the problem, have all three experimenters test an equal number of people in each major.

2. Confound #1. subject selection: there is a comparison being made between volunteers and non-volunteers; the volunteers for the new procedure might be more open to new ideas and perhaps less anxious; it would be better to ask for volunteers who would be willing to test this new procedure, with the understanding that some would be randomly assigned to the new approach, while others would be randomly assigned to the traditional approach.

   Confound #2. the doctors: the more experienced and perhaps the more competent doctors are being assigned to the new procedure; as with the patients, doctors should be informed of the new procedure, asked if they would like to participate in evaluating it, with the understanding that they could be assigned to either the new or the old procedure; the researchers should take steps to insure that the level of experience is the same in both conditions.

3. Confound #1. sequence: participants locate the four buildings in the same order; it's possible that having located the chapel, locating the gym will be easier (or harder); to correct the problem, the locations should be presented in a random order; also, it would be best to give the participant four blank maps, one of each location; that way, on every trial the participant would start with a map that has only the psychology building located

   Confound #2. the north orientation: the north orientation is given with just two of the locations; it should be given with all of the locations for some of the participants and with none of the locations with other participants.

4. Confound #1. class time. Assuming students can decide which class to take, the 8:00 class might have different types of students in it than the 2:00 class; this is a hard problem to solve in real world educational research, but it would be ideal to have two sections of the class at about the same time.

   Confound #2. student work. In addition to having the study guide, students in the 8:00 class are completing homework assignments, while those in the 2:00 class aren't doing anything comparable; to correct the problem, those in the 2:00 class should have some type of homework assignment, to equate the groups in terms of "amount of out of class time thinking about the course."

   Confound #3. teacher expectations. There is a third problem here and that is the teacher's bias about the effectiveness of the study guide; it is possible that the teacher might "teach harder" in the 8:00 class; this is difficult to solve, because it is hard to find anyone without any preconceived notions about the effectiveness of study guides, and it is probably impractical for the researcher to recruit two non-biased colleagues and randomly assign them to the two conditions; the best the researcher can probably do is to (a) insure that the tests given in the course are standardized and identical for the two groups, (b) be aware of potential bias and compulsively guard against having it affect day-to-day behavior.

Chapter 6. Control Problems in Experimental Research

Reviewing the Main Concepts
After you finish reading and studying each main section of the chapter, answer the following questions to test your comprehension. The numbers in parentheses after each question are the page numbers in the text that will help you with the answer.

- *Between-Subjects Designs*
  - The "Barbara Helm" study is a good example of a situation in which a between-subjects design must be used. Explain. (181)

  - Aside from a "Barbara Helm" type of study, in what other circumstance is a between-subjects design normally used instead of a within-subjects design? (180)

  - Other than the problem of equivalent groups, what is a disadvantage of using a between-subjects design? (181)

- *The Problem of Creating Equivalent Groups*
  - In a between-subjects design, why is it important to aim for equivalent groups? (181-182)

  - What is the difference between random selection and random assignment? (182)

- Explain how random assignment accomplishes the goal of creating equivalent groups. (182-183)

- Random assignment is often accomplished through block randomization. What does this procedure guarantee? (183)

- What are the conditions under which matching is preferred to random assignment? (185-187)

- What determines which variables will become "matching" variables? (187)

- *Within-Subjects Designs*
  - What are the advantages of within-subjects designs over between-subjects designs? What is the main problem that a within-subjects design has to solve? (187-190)

  - What is the difference between a progressive effect and a carryover effect? (190)

- *The Problem of Controlling Sequence Effects*
    - o   What is the general purpose of counterbalancing? (191)

    - o   What is "complete" counterbalancing? If there are five different conditions in a study, how many sequences will be needed if complete counterbalancing is going to be used? (191-192)

    - o   What is "partial" counterbalancing? What are two ways to accomplish partial counterbalancing? (192-193)

    - o   What are the unique features of a Latin square? (192-193)

    - o   If you test each condition more than once in a within-subjects design, what are two ways of accomplishing counterbalancing? (193-195)

    - o   Consider the Carello study, which examined a participant's ability to judge dowel length from sound. Explain how she used block randomization to accomplish counterbalancing. (195-196) o   Explain what is meant by asymmetric transfer. If it is likely to be a problem in an experiment, how might it be eliminated? ( )

- *Control Problems in Developmental Research*
  - o   What is a cross-sectional design? (196-198)

  - o   What are cohort effects and how might they make the interpretation of cross-sectional designs difficult? (198-199)

  - o   What is a longitudinal design and what methodological problem occurs with this type of design? (198)

  - o   Describe how Terman's famous research on giftedness avoided the major problem with longitudinal designs. (200-201)

- *Problems with Biasing*
  - o   What is experimenter bias and how can it be demonstrated experimentally? (201)

  - o   What are two ways to control experimenter bias? (203)

o   What is the Hawthorne effect (as it is traditionally defined)? (204)

o   Contrary to what has traditionally been described as happening at the Hawthorne plant, what actually happened there? (204-205)

o   What is the good subject effect, how does it relate to demand characteristics, and how might it influence the outcome of a study? (205-206)

o   Give an example of how evaluation apprehension might influence the outcome of a study. (206)

o   How can participant bias be controlled? (206-207)

Key Terms
Each of the following terms will be (a) printed in boldface in the chapter, and (b) found in the glossary at the end of the text. After you finish reading and studying the chapter, try to write definitions of each or examples that illustrate each. In parentheses after each term I've put the page on which it first appears.

Between-subjects design (180)

Within-subjects design (180)

Equivalent groups (181)

Random assignment (182)

Block randomization (183)

Matching (185)

Matching variable (185)

Sequence (order) effect (190)

Progressive effect (190)

Carryover effect (190)

Counterbalancing (191)

Complete counterbalancing (191)

Partial counterbalancing (192)

Latin square (192)

Reverse counterbalancing (194)

Asymmetric transfer (197)

Cross-sectional study (198)

Longitudinal study (198)

Cohort effect (198)

Experimenter bias (201)

Double-blind (203)

Participant bias (204)

Hawthorne effect (204)

Good subject effect (205)

Demand characteristics (205)

Evaluation apprehension (206)

Manipulation check (206)

Sample Test Items

<u>Fill-ins</u>

The answers to these fill-in-the-blank questions can be found in the list of key terms.

1. In a taste test, Joan is asked to evaluate diet drinks in the following order: Diet Coke, Diet Pepsi, Diet Pepsi, Diet Coke. The researcher is using the method of _____ counterbalancing.

2. Concern over _____ effects might cause a developmental psychologist to use a longitudinal design instead of a cross-sectional design.

3. Random assignment and matching are two procedures used for the purpose of trying to create _____.

4. Although this does not appear to be what really happened at Western Electric, the concept of the _____ effect has come to mean that participant behaviors can be influenced by the mere fact that they know they are in an experiment.

5. _____ procedures are often used in research to avoid experimenter bias; these procedures also reduce participant bias.

6. Using the technique of _____, an experimenter presenting 4 different words to participants used 24 different sequences.

7. Fatigue and boredom are examples of order effects that are known as _____ effects.

8. Any aspect of a procedure that gives away the true research hypothesis is called a

_____.

Matching

Terms in the left-hand column are key terms. For each term, find the correct matching example or concept description or example, and write in the letter of the term in the blank space.

A. good subject effect   _____   controlled by automating procedures

B. experimenter bias   _____   form of partial counterbalancing

C. block randomization   _____   Terman's is the classic example

D. reverse counterbalancing   _____   tries to support experimenter's hypothesis

E. asymmetric transfer   _____   use when extraneous factor correlates with DV

F. Latin square   _____   alternative to reverse counterbalancing

G. longitudinal study   _____   between-subjects design

H. cross-sectional study   _____   if present, counterbalancing might fail

I. matching   _____   works best with large N

J. random assignment   _____   1234554321

Multiple Choice

1. Compared with between-subjects designs, within-subjects designs
    a. require the testing of a greater number of participants
    b. are more likely to require matching
    c. are the only designs for which a block randomization procedure can be used
    d. must solve the problem of sequence effects

2. In a between-subjects design, if there is a difference in performance found between the two groups, that difference could be due to any of the following factors except
    a. the sequence in which the groups were tested
    b. chance
    c. the participants in one group are just better than those in the other group
    d. the independent variable had its predicted effect

3. As a means of creating equivalent groups, when is random assignment preferred over matching?
    a. when large N is available
    b. any time the researcher suspects that some extraneous variable might correlate with the dependent variable
    c. whenever participants are only going to be tested once per condition rather than twice per condition
    d. none of the above – matching is always preferred if the researcher has the time to do it

4. In order to accomplish random assignment and insure that an equal number of participants are tested in each of the groups, the researcher would be well advised to use
    a. a Latin square
    b. block randomization
    c. random selection
    d. a manipulation check

5. Which of the following is true about counterbalancing?
    a. if participants are to be tested just once per condition, reverse counterbalancing is the ideal option
    b. it works better for carryover effects than for progressive effects
    c. in between-subjects designs, it is used to insure that each condition has been tested once, before any condition is tested a second time
    d. if there are six different levels of the independent variable, partial counterbalancing is preferred over complete counterbalancing

6. In some within-subjects perception experiments, participants are tested many times per condition. Over the course of 45 minutes in such an experiment, they might become bored. This tendency is known as
    a. a progressive effect
    b. a demand characteristic
    c. a Hawthorne effect
    d. a carryover effect

7. Which of the following is true about asymmetric transfer?
    a. if strongly suspected, it might be better to switch to a between-subjects design
    b. more likely with progressive effects than with carryover effects
    c. requires complete counterbalancing; partial won't due
    d. solved with a double blind procedure

8. In the Reynolds study of expert chess players, 15 different persons each evaluated six different chess boards. What form of counterbalancing was used?
    a. complete
    b. reverse
    c. partial
    d. Latin square

9. Which of the following is true about the case study by Carello, in which students estimated the lengths of dowels by listening to them hit the floor?
    a. she used hearing ability as a matching variable
    b. she used block randomization to determine the sequence of presenting the various dowel lengths
    c. each dowel length was tested just once and complete counterbalancing was used
    d. the length of the dowel to be dropped was determined by a Latin square

10. _____ effects sometimes make it difficult for developmental psychologists to interpret the results of cross-sectional studies.
    a. Cohort
    b. Sequence
    c. Attrition
    d. Good subject

11. One of the reasons for using deception in research is to
    a. eliminate experimenter bias
    b. reduce the likelihood of demand characteristics
    c. avoid evaluation apprehension
    d. eliminate the so-called Hawthorne effect

12. In a study on the effects of crowding on problem solving, some participants were interrupted in the middle of the procedure and asked a series of questions to determine if the crowding conditions were stressful for them. At that point their participation ended. What was the purpose of the interruption?
    a. it was a manipulation check
    b. it was designed to reduce participant bias
    c. it was designed to eliminate those playing the role of "good subject"
    d. it was designed to see if the interruption would reduce the number of problems solved

Applications Exercise

6.1. Between or Within?

For each of the following, first identify the independent and dependent variables (in general terms). Then decide whether it would be more appropriate to use a between-subjects design or a within-subjects design, given the limited information presented for each study. Explain your choice. If you think a between-subjects design is called for, decide whether equivalent groups could be formed and if so, the best way to form them (random assignment or matching). If you think matching is needed, identify a matching variable. If you think a within-subjects design is called for, then make a recommendation about the type of counterbalancing to use.

1. In study of eyewitness memory, a researcher wishes to determine whether the accuracy of eyewitness memory can be influenced by the level of stress an eyewitness experiences.

2. In a cross-cultural study of prejudice, a researcher wished to know whether prejudices would develop earlier in life for Western (e.g., United States) or Eastern (e.g., China) cultures.

3. In a study on the sense of touch, blindfolded participants had to judge whether the apparatus touching their skin had two points or one. The researcher wished to determine if different areas of the skin (e.g., palm of the hand vs. small of the back) were differentially sensitive.

4. A cognitive psychologist interested in the development of memory studies (annually) the short-term memory capacity of the same 20 children as they grow from age 4 through age 8.

5. To determine whether there is a universality to facial expressions of emotions, a researcher prepares pictures of people from three different cultures, each showing the same variety of expressions (e.g., smile, scowl). On a given trial of the study, a participant looks at a photo, then chooses a matching emotion from a list of ten different emotions.

6. A psychologist interested in mazes wishes to learn whether learning is faster when the maze is run 10 times a day, once a day for ten 10 days, or twice a day for five days.

Answers to Sample Test Items

Fill-ins

    1. reverse
    2. cohort
    3. equivalent groups
    4. Hawthorne
    5. Double blind
    6. complete counterbalancing
    7. progressive
    8. demand characteristic

Matching

    From top to bottom, the correct letter sequence is: B, F, G, A, I, C, H, E, J, D

Multiple Choice

1. a. within-subjects designs require fewer participants
   b. matching is a procedure for creating equivalent groups in between-subjects designs
   c. block randomization procedure is indeed a counterbalancing option, but it can also be used in between-subjects designs as a means of accomplishing random assignment
   d. CORRECT ANSWER – and these effects are dealt with through the various forms of counterbalancing

2. a. CORRECT ANSWER - unless it introduces some systematic confound, this shouldn't matter; sequence is the problem for within-subjects designs, not between-subjects designs
   b. this is always a possibility, even though it might be a remote one (i.e., <.05)
   c. this is possible, although one would hope that random assignment would have created equivalent groups
   d. this of course is the desired outcome

3. a. CORRECT ANSWER - unless there are overwhelming indications that matching should be used, large N makes it almost certain that random assignment will create equivalent groups
   b. if this happens, then matching is preferred
   c. both these situations occur only in within-subjects designs
   d. matching should only be used when there is a strong suspicion that some factor correlates with the DV and that factor can be measured

4. a. this is a means of counterbalancing in within-subjects designs
   b. CORRECT ANSWER - each "block" contains a randomized sequence of the different conditions being tested
   c. random selection has to do with how participants are initially selected for a study, not how they are assigned to groups
   d. this is a procedure done to insure the independent variable is working properly and to check for participant bias

5. a. reverse counterbalancing is an option when participants are tested more than once per condition
   b. the opposite is true
   c. it isn't used in between-subjects designs
   d. CORRECT ANSWER – complete counterbalancing in this case would require 720 different sequences (6!); partial counterbalancing (e.g., Latin square) would be more practical

6. a. CORRECT ANSWER – the boredom "progressively" builds during the session
   b. this is some aspect of the study that gives away the true hypothesis
   c. this is when behavior is influenced simply by the knowledge that one is in an experiment
   d. this is another type of sequence effect

7. a. CORRECT ANSWER – because in this case, counterbalancing might not solve the problem
   b. the opposite is true
   c. both forms of counterbalancing might fail if asymmetric transfer exists
   d. useful in avoiding experimenter bias; irrelevant here

8. a. six boards would require 720 different sequences (6!) and he only had 15 participants
   b. each person was tested just once, not more than once
   c. CORRECT ANSWER – he used a random sample of the 720 possible sequences
   d. this would mean a 6x6 square and he would have needed either six participants or some multiple of six (to insure an equal number of participants per row of the square)

9. a. this was a within-subjects design
   b. CORRECT ANSWER – each dowels length was tested one time, in random sequence, before any of the dowel lengths were tested for a second time
   c. each dowel length was tested several times
   d. a Latin square was not used in this study

10. a. CORRECT ANSWER - this is especially true if the different groups are far apart in age (e.g., 10 years)
    b. this is a problem for within-subjects designs and a cross-sectional design is a between-subjects design
    c. this is a problem for developmental psychologists using longitudinal designs
    d. this could be a problem in any kind of designs, not just a cross-sectional study

11. a. the experimenter would still know the hypothesis and bias could still occur
    b. CORRECT ANSWER – deception reduces the chance of there being cues present in the procedure that give away the true purpose
    c. regardless of whether deception is used, some participants will experience this anyway
    d. participants will still know they are in an experiment and that knowledge might affect them in some way

12. a. CORRECT ANSWER – the researchers were probably expecting problem solving ability to decline when it was crowded, presumably because participants would feel stressed in the crowding room; it's a good idea to check and see if the small room indeed produced feelings of stress it was a manipulation check
    b. procedures to reduce participant bias (e.g., deception) occur for participants who complete the whole procedure and have their data included in the final analysis
    c. this problem is hard to avoid, and a manipulation check won't do the job
    d. these participants left the experiment after the manipulation check; there wouldn't be any data for them

Feedback on Applications Exercise

Between or Within?

1. IV = stress levels experienced
   DV = eyewitness accuracy
   Between-subjects design: presumably there will be at least two levels of stress and a participant will witness some kind of event unexpectedly then have to report on it; having done this once, it would be impractical to have the same person do it again when experiencing a different level of stress.
   Equivalent groups: use random assignment if there is a large participant pool; otherwise, it might be wise to match the groups on their characteristic levels of anxiety, as determined by a test for anxiety tendencies.

2. IVs = culture and age
   DV = level of prejudice
   Between-subjects design: both independent variables are subject variables, thereby dictating a between-subjects approach; because the groups are inherently nonequivalent
   Equivalent groups: neither random assignment nor matching could be used to create equivalent groups (you will learn in Chapter 7, however, that a form of matching is often used in designs like this to reduce the degree of nonequivalency)

3. IV = area of the skin
   DV = judgment (one or two points)
   Within-subjects design: like most research in sensation and perception, this is a situation in which participating in one condition (palm being tested) won't have much of an effect on being tested in the other condition (back), as long as counterbalancing is used properly; also, in this type of study it is important for each person to make a comparison between his or her palm and back.
   Counterbalancing: each position would probably be tested several times; either reverse counterbalancing or block randomization could be used; because there are only two positions being tested, another option would be to simply alternate from one to another.

4. IV = age
   DV = STM capacity
   Within-subjects design: by studying the same children every year, this is a longitudinal design.
   Counterbalancing: not relevant of course (unless the researcher has a time machine that would enable him or her to test a child first at age 8 then at age 6, etc.)

5. IV = cultures represented in the photos
   DV = accuracy of judging the emotion
   Within-subjects: it would be good to see if the same participant could accurately judge a particular emotion (e.g. sadness) when displayed in three different cultures.
   Counterbalancing: let's say there are 21 photos - seven emotions shown for each of the three cultures; if each participant is tested once, partial counterbalancing would be used, probably by giving each participant a random sequence of the photos; if testing occurred more than once per participant, block randomization would probably be used (several consecutive random sequences of the 21 faces)

6. IV = maze running schedule
   DV = learning
   Between-subjects: once a rat has been tested in one of the three conditions, that rat "knows" the maze; rats should begin each of the three conditions in a state of maze ignorance.
   Equivalent groups: white rats are very similar genetically and cheap to buy or raise; random assignment will be fine here.

Chapter 7. Experimental Design I: Single-Factor Designs

Reviewing the Main Concepts
After you finish reading and studying each main section of the chapter, answer the following questions to test your comprehension. The numbers in parentheses after each question are the page numbers in the text that will help you with the answer.

- *Single-Factor – Two Levels*
  - o Identify the defining feature of a single-factor independent groups design and describe the case study example in the chapter. (215-216)

  - o Why was a matched groups design used in the case study on sleep deprivation and what was the matching variable used? (217-218)

  - o Use the case study on giftedness to explain why the conclusions drawn from nonequivalent groups designs are non-causal. (218)

  - o Describe the Stroop effect and explain why his first two studies were examples of single factor repeated-measures designs. (219-220)

  - o Describe the reason for the particular counterbalancing procedure used by Lee and Aronson in their study of motion perception in children. (221-222)

o Identify the situations when a *t* test for independent groups will be used and when a *t* test for dependent groups will be used. (222-223)

- *Control Group Designs*
    o What is a placebo and what is the reason for including a placebo control group in an experiment? (223-224)

    o When are waiting list control groups used and why are they used? (224-226)

    o In the case study of subliminal self-help audiotapes, what did the two types of control groups enable the researchers to conclude about the effectiveness of the tapes? (226-227)

    o Use the Weiss study on the control of tail shock to illustrate the use of a yoked control group. (227-229)

    o Using control groups to evaluate the effectiveness of some new therapy or program is sometimes controversial. Why is this so and what is the defense of control groups made by researchers? (225-226)

- *Single Factor – More than Two Levels*
  - o Use the Ebbinghaus forgetting curve to illustrate an advantage of having more than two levels of an independent variable. (231-232)

  - o Consider the Bransford and Johnson study on the effects of context on memory. The purpose of adding the additional groups was not to find nonlinear effects. What was the reason? (230, 232-234)

  - o Describe how a multi-level repeated-measures design was used to assess the so-called Mozart effect. (234-235)

  - o When presenting results, when is a table preferred over a graph? (236)

  - o When presenting a graph of the Bransford and Johnson study, why must it be a bar graph and not a line graph? (236-237)

  - o What is the problem with using multiple t tests to analyze the results from a multilevel groups design? What should be done instead? (238-239)

Key Terms
Each of the following terms will be (a) printed in boldface in the chapter, and (b) found in the glossary at the end of the text. After you finish reading and studying the chapter, try to write definitions of each or examples that illustrate each. In parentheses after each term I've put the page on which it first appears.

Independent groups design (215)

Matched groups design (215)

Nonequivalent groups design (215)

Repeated-measures design (215)

t test for independent groups (222)

t test for dependent groups (223)

Placebo control group (223)

Waiting list control group (224)

Yoked control group (227)

Single-factor multilevel design (229)

Nonlinear effects (229)

Continuous variable (236)

Discrete variable (237)

ANOVA (239)

Sample Test Items

<u>Fill-ins</u>

The answers to these fill-in-the-blank questions can be found in the list of key terms.

1. If a graph includes points connected by straight lines, rather than a series of bars, then the independent variable on the X-axis is most likely to be a _____ variable.

2. If a study has just one independent variable, adding more than two levels provides the opportunity to discover _____ effects.

3. In a study comparing two kinds of intellectual puzzles that differ in their level of complexity, the researcher worries that the IQ levels of the participants might be correlated with the dependent variable. In the case, it would be wise to use a _____ design.

4. A _____ control group is especially likely to be found in research evaluating the effectiveness of some new type of therapy.

5. A single factor experiment that uses a subject variable is referred to as a _____ design.

6. When the behavior of a participant in the experimental group affects what happens to a participant in the control group, the study is using a _____ control group.

7. Studies with two levels of a repeated-measures independent variable would be statistically analyzed by using a *t* test for _____.

8. Random assignment of participants to two groups is the defining feature of the _____ design.

Matching

Terms in the left-hand column are key terms. For each term, find the correct matching example or concept description or example, and write in the letter of the term in the blank space.

A. ANOVA   _____ analysis for single-factor, two level design

B. nonlinear effect   _____ treatment depends on experimental group

C. discrete variable   _____ whenever a subject variable is used

D. yoked control group   _____ within-subjects design

E. placebo control group   _____ allows for a line graph

F. *t* test, independent groups   _____ participants eventually get treatment

G. nonequivalent groups design   _____ Ebbinghaus forgetting curve for example

H. repeated-measures design   _____ gender for example

I. continuous variable   _____ analysis for multilevel design

J. waiting list control group   _____ often used to evaluate drug/alcohol effects

Multiple Choice

1. How does an independent groups design (IGD) differ from a nonequivalent groups design (NGD)?
   a. IGD has two levels of the independent variable; NGD is a multilevel design
   b. IGD can use matching; matching cannot be used in NGD
   c. because an IGD can use repeated measures, fewer participants are needed for this design than for an NGD
   d. subject variables will be found in NGD but not in IGD

2. The matched groups study by Blagrove attempted to see if sleep deprivation could make people more susceptible to leading questions. What was the matching variable?
   a. the amount of sleep typically experienced by participants
   b. whether or not participants experienced sleep deprivation
   c. the verbal abilities of the participants
   d. whether or not participants had experienced being in a real courtroom, being asked leading questions by lawyers

3. Which of the following case studies used a repeated-measures design?
   a. the Lee and Aronson study of the effects of a moving room on children's balance
   b. the Blakemore and Cooper study on the effects of cats in vertical or horizontal environments
   c. the Merickle and Skanes study that used placebos and waiting lists to evaluate subliminal self-help tapes
   d. the Bransford and Johnson study of the effects of context on memory

4. Stroop completed three experiments, the second one demonstrating his famous "Stroop effect." Which of the following was true about that study?
   a. he used a nonequivalent groups design
   b. he used a multilevel as opposed to a two-level design
   c. he used a repeated-measures design
   d. he presented the conditions in different sequences using a Latin square

5. A researcher wishes to see if using imagery can improve memory. Participants in an experimental group are trained to use imagery, and then given a 30-item list of words to learn. Words are presented one at a time and then recalled, so people in this group vary in terms of how many times they have to study the list before they know it. Control group participants will just repeat the words to themselves as the words are presented. What would be the best type of control group to use here?
   a. a placebo control group
   b. a yoked control group
   c. a waiting list control group
   d. none of the above – a simple control group that is shown the words once will be fine

6. The famous Ebbinghaus study that investigated the rate of forgetting over time is an example of which of the following methodological points?
   a. using multiple t tests increases the chances of making a Type I error
   b. adding levels of an independent variable allows for the discovery of a nonlinear effect
   c. adding different groups in a multilevel strategy allows alternative hypotheses to be ruled out
   d. bar graphs are called for when the dependent variable is a discrete variable

7. Concerning the decision about whether to use bar graphs or line graphs,
   a. if the X-axis contains a discrete variable, a bar graph should be used
   b. if the X-axis contains a discrete variable, a line graph should be used
   c. if the X-axis contains a continuous variable, a bar graph must be used
   d. if the X-axis contains a continuous variable, a line graph must be used

8. A waiting list control group is most likely to appear in a study
   a. examining the effects of caffeine on steadiness
   b. evaluating the effects of systematic desensitization therapy on the reduction of phobias
   c. studying the influence of control on stress (as in the Weiss study with the rats)
   d. comparing males and females in their ability to not get lost

9. Which of the following is true about a study like the Bransford and Johnson study of the effects of context (the sketch of the man serenading the woman with a guitar) on memory?
   a. the analysis would involve a t test for independent groups rather than a t test for dependent groups
   b. they added levels to the independent variable in order to find a nonlinear effect
   c. data analysis calls for a 1-way Analysis of Variance
   d. the data could be presented either in a table or as a line graph

10. A researcher is interested in studying the effects of alcohol on reaction time. Participants are randomly assigned to an experimental group, a placebo control group, and a straight control group. Average reaction time in the experimental group is .36 sec. Which of the following average scores for the other two groups would allow the researcher to conclude that the apparent effect of alcohol was nothing but a placebo effect?
   a. the placebo group = .36 sec. and the straight control = .23 sec.
   b. the placebo group = .30 sec. and the straight control = .23 sec.
   c. the placebo group = .23 sec. and the straight control = .23 sec.
   d. the placebo group = .36 sec. and the straight control = .36 sec.

11. Control groups are sometimes criticized on ethical grounds – in research on therapy effectiveness, for instance, it is sometimes argued that people might be denied an effective way to solve their problems by being placed in a no-treatment control group. Researchers reply in several ways. Which of the following is *not* one of them?
    a. control groups simply aren't used when testing the effectiveness of therapy
    b. control group members often get an existing therapy (rather than the experimental therapy); they aren't denied therapy completely
    c. whether people would be denied a truly "effective" therapy cannot be known without completing methodologically sound (i.e., proper control groups) research
    d. in studies with waiting lists, the therapy is eventually available to control group members

12. When would a researcher be more likely to present data in a table rather than in a graph?
    a. whenever there are two levels rather than multiple levels of the independent variable
    b. when the researcher wants to convey the precise values of the means
    c. whenever the independent variable involves a discrete variable rather than a continuous variable
    d. none of the above – in fact, the best strategy is to present the same data both in a table and in a graph

Applications Exercises

7.1. Identifying Experimental Designs

For each of the following, identify the independent variable and its levels, and the dependent variable. For the independent variable, indicate whether it is (a) a between- or a within-subjects variable, and (b) a manipulated or a subject variable. For the dependent variable(s), identify the measurement scale. Finally, identify the experimental design for each study.

1. In a study of the effects of motivation on maze-running speed, 50 rats are tested in a 20-foot alley maze (i.e., no turns, just a straight run from one end to the other). Some rats perform the task after going 5 hours without food, others after going 10 hours without food, and others after going 15 hours without food. Rats are placed in the different conditions in such a way as to insure that the average weights of the rats in all conditions are equal.

2. In a cross-cultural study of helping behavior, researchers ask local residents for directions to the train station. The study takes place in London, Paris, Berlin, and Rome.

3. In a study of food preferences, participants taste a series of six different rice dishes, each seasoned differently, and rate each (on 5-point scales) for (a) intensity of the taste and (b) the pleasantness of the taste.

4. In a study of the effects of interference on memory, some students study a list of words (list A) for 20 minutes, then study a second list (list B) for 20 minutes, then try to recall the words on list A. Other students study list A for 20 minutes, then take a 20-minute break, then try to recall the words on list A.

5. A developmental psychologist wishes to study how memory ability develops during early and middle childhood. Children in the first, third, and fifth grades are given a digit span test (experimenter reads a sequence of numbers; participates recites them back in the same order).

6. A motivational psychologist wonders if rankings of food advertisements will be influenced by hunger levels. College students who have not eaten for either 6 or 12 hours are shown ten print ads and are asked to place them in a pile so that the "best ad" (however they define it) is on top, the next best is next, and so on.

7.2. Portraying Research Results

For each of the following studies, create a graph that most accurately portrays the results. Be sure to make proper decisions about whether a bar or a line graph would be more appropriate.

1. On the Stroop test, participants are shown a list of color words printed in mismatched colors (e.g., the word red printed in green ink) and their task is to name the color the word has been printed in (e.g., "green"). It is a confusing task and the researcher hypothesizes that people will do even worse than they usually do if they are under the influence of caffeine. Participants are randomly assigned to a caffeine group, a placebo group, and a control group.

    Outcome A. The hypothesis is supported.

    Outcome B. The hypothesis is not supported – the caffeine group does poorly, but the result is nothing more than a placebo effect.

2. In a voice recognition study, participants listen to a recorded message (the target voice), then a "voice lineup," a series of brief messages spoken by several speakers, including the target speaker. Their task is to correctly identify the target voice. The independent variable is the length of the initial message read by the target voice – it lasts 10 seconds, 20 seconds, or 30 seconds. The researcher hypothesizes that recognition accuracy will increase as a linear function of the length of the target voice message.

    Outcome A. The hypothesis is supported.

Outcome B. The hypothesis is only partially supported – accuracy doesn't improve
significantly until the voice message reaches 30 seconds in length.

3. A sports psychologist hypothesizes that basketball players will perform best if their motivation
is very high. Players are randomly assigned to three groups varying in level of motivation and
then shoot 30 foul shots. Those in the low motivation group are simply told they should get at
least 20 out of 30 and if they don't they will have to run two laps around the court. Those in the
moderate motivation group are told that if they don't get 20 out of 30, they will be running four
laps, Those in the high motivation are told that a failure to achieve 20 of 30 will result in their
having to run eight laps.

Outcome A. The hypothesis is supported – the higher the motivation, the better the
performance.

Outcome B. The hypothesis is not supported, performance is only good at moderate levels of
motivation.

Answers to Sample Test Items

Fill-ins

1. continuous
2. nonlinear
3. matched groups
4. waiting list
5. nonequivalent groups
6. yoked
7. dependent groups
8. independent groups

Matching

From top to bottom, the correct letter sequence is: F, D, G, H, I, J, B, C, A, E

Multiple Choice

1. a. both types of designs can be either two-level or multilevel
   b. a matched group design is a different type of design from both IGD and NGD; with NGD however, researchers often try to equate the groups as much as possible on a number of variables
   c. an IGD does not use repeated measures
   d. CORRECT ANSWER – the presence of subject variables defines the NGD

2. a. CORRECT ANSWER –groups were matched in terms of "self-reported habitual sleep duration"
   b. this was the independent variable
   c. this might possibly have influenced the results, but Blagrove did not use it for matching
   d. not especially relevant

3. a. CORRECT ANSWER – the children experienced the room moving forward *and* backward
   b. this was an independent groups study (in general, the word "or" tells you the answer – if cats experience one thing or the other, they aren't experiencing both)
   c. these types of controls (placebo, waiting list) imply the existence of different groups
   d. this is a good example of a study that could not have been run as a repeated-measures study – once participants have studied and recalled the material, they really cannot do it again under a different level of the independent variable

4. a. participants completed both the Stroop condition and the control condition
   b. he used a two-level design
   c. CORRECT ANSWER
   d. he used a reverse counterbalancing procedure

5. a. this type of group is best used in situations in which you want participants to think they are experiencing some effect (e.g., alcohol) but really aren't
   b. CORRECT ANSWER – if two experimental group participants use, say, 6 and 8 trials to learn the list, there ought to be two control group participants who study the list (without imagery) for 6 and 8 trials
   c. this type of group is best used in situations in which you want participants to similar to the people who are getting treatment
   d. those in the experimental group are studying the lists varying number of times; that needs to be true of those in the control group also

6. a. actually, the Ebbinghaus studies were completed before *t* tests were invented
   b. CORRECT ANSWER –and a nonlinear effect is just what Ebbinghaus found
   c. this is another reason for adding levels, but not the reason used by Ebbinghaus
   d. this is true, but Ebbinghaus used a continuous variable (time between learning a list and relearning it

7. a. CORRECT ANSWER
   b. a line graph implies intermediate points, which don't exist with discrete variables
   c. with a continuous variable, line graphs are normally used, but a bar graph could be used
   d. with a continuous variable, line graphs are normally used

8. a. this calls for a placebo control group
   b. CORRECT ANSWER – waiting list controls are typically used in studies evaluating therapy; this creates two groups with similar problems
   c. this calls for a yoked control group
   d. this type of study does not have a control group per se

9. a. because it is a multilevel design, neither type of *t* test is appropriate
   b. they added levels to rule out alternative hypotheses
   c. CORRECT ANSWER
   d a table would be fine, but a bar graph is called for here (discrete variable on the X-axis)

10. a. CORRECT ANSWER – expecting alcohol yields exactly the same results as actually getting alcohol
    b. this suggests both a true effect of alcohol (.36 minus .30) and a partial placebo effect (.30 minus .23)
    c. this indicates no placebo effect at all, but a clear effect due to alcohol
    d. this indicates no effect of either a placebo or the alcohol

11. a. CORRECT ANSWER - waiting list control groups or groups given another form of therapy are normally used in this kind of research, so this argument would not be made
    b. this argument is frequently made
    c. this argument is also made
    d. so is this one

12. a. with just two levels, the data would best be presented as a graph or perhaps just verbally, worked into a sentence in the results section of the report
    b. CORRECT ANSWER – exact values usually have to be guessed at with a graph
    c. irrelevant – this distinction relates to the decision about whether to use a line or a bar graph
    d. actually, this is the one thing you should never do

Feedback on Applications Exercises

Identifying Experimental Designs

1. IV: hours of deprivation (levels = 5, 10, 15)
      between-subjects; manipulated
   DV: time to run maze (ratio)
   Design: single-factor, multilevel, matched groups design (matching variable = weight)

2. IV: city location (levels = London, Paris, Berlin, and Rome)
      between-subjects; subject (local residents)
   DV: whether help is given or not (nominal)
   Design: single-factor, multilevel, nonequivalent groups design

3. IV: food type (levels = the six different types of rice)
      within-subjects; manipulated
   DV: ratings for intensity and quality (both interval)
   Design: single-factor, multilevel, repeated-measures design

4. IV: study sequence (levels = A then B, A then rest)
      between-subjects; manipulated
   DV: words recalled (ratio)
   Design: single-factor, two level, independent groups design

5. IV: grade in school (levels = 1st, 3rd, 5th)
      between-subjects; subject
   DV: score on digit span task (ratio)
   Design: single-factor, multilevel, nonequivalent groups design

6. IV: hunger level (levels = 6 or 12 hours without food)
      between-subjects; manipulated
   DV: rankings of the magazine ads (ordinal)
   Design: single-factor, two-level, independent groups design

Displaying Research Results

1. Outcome A. The three groups reflect discrete categories, so a bar graph is needed. If caffeine is the only factor hindering performance, then the bar for the caffeine group will be high (high score means more time to complete the task) and the other two will be lower and equal to each other.

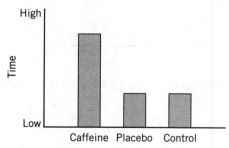

Outcome B. If it is only a placebo effect, then the placebo group and the caffeine group will perform the same and worse (higher) than the straight control group.

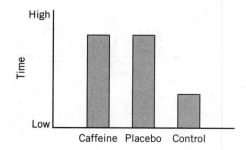

2. Outcome A. The duration of the target voice is a continuous variable, so a line graph can be used. Recognition accuracy increases steadily as the voice duration increases

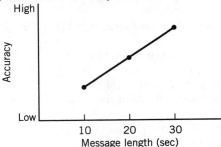

Outcome B. Performance is best at the longest voice duration (30 sec); the other two are the same.

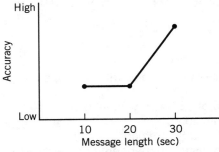

3. Outcome A. Number of laps is a continuous variable, but the values chosen, 2, 4, and 8 laps, don't represent equal increments. Hence a bar graph is better on this one. If the hypothesis is supported, then shooting accuracy increases steadily with increased motivation

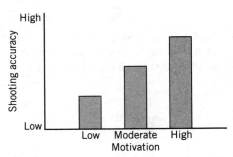

Outcome B. In this case, performance is best for the intermediate level of motivation and poor for both high and low motivation.

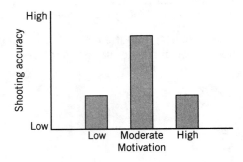

Chapter 8. Experimental Design II: Factorial Designs

Reviewing the Main Concepts
After you finish reading and studying each main section of the chapter, answer the following questions to test your comprehension. The numbers in parentheses after each question are the page numbers in the text that will help you with the answer.

- *Factorial Essentials*
    - Using a 2x4 design as an example, explain how the factorial notation system tells you the number of independent variables in an experiment, the number of levels of each independent variable, and the total number of conditions in the study. (246-247)

    - In an experiment with one independent variable, the number of "levels" and the number of "conditions" amount to the same thing. This is no longer true in a factorial study. Explain. (247)

- *Outcomes – Main Effects and Interactions*
    - What is a main effect? How many main effects can occur on a 2x3x4 factorial study? (249-250)

    - What are row and column means and what do they have to do with the concept of a main effect? (250)

o   In the case study on imagery and memory, what were the two factors and which produced a significant main effect? (251-252)

o   What is an interaction effect? (253-254)

o   Use Godden and Baddeley's study of the Scottish diving club as a way to show that an experiment can have no main effects but a significant interaction. (254-255)

o   What is a ceiling effect and how can it affect the interpretation of a research outcome? (257)

o   When main effects and an interaction both occur in a study, interactions should be examined and interpreted first. Why? (267-258)

o   Describe how the general look of a graph can indicate the presence or absence of an interaction. (258)

- The famous Jenkins and Dallenbach study on retroactive interference was a 2x4 factorial. What was the "2" and the "4" and what was the outcome of the study? (259-262)

- Varieties of Factorial Designs
  - What is the defining feature of a mixed factorial design? (262)

  - In a mixed factorial, counterbalancing is not always needed. Use the two case studies to explain. (263-266)

  - What is the defining feature of a PxE factorial design? How does its name relate to the famous psychologist Kurt Lewin? (262, 269-270)

  - Use the large room/small room, introvert/extravert example to show how one type of main effect in a PxE design tells you something important about how people differ. (267)

  - Use the large room/small room, introvert/extravert example to show how one type of main effect in a PxE design tells you something important about how some situations can be powerful enough to overcome individual differences. (267)

o Use the large room/small room, introvert/extravert example to show how to interpret an outcome with no main effects but a significant PxE interaction. (267-268)

o What is an ATI and why is it important in, say, educational research? (268-269)

o Describe the outcome of the case study with a PxE interaction (compared Type A and Type B persons). (269-270)

o Consider a 2x2 factorial that is (a) an independent groups factorial, (b) a mixed factorial, and (c) a repeated-measures factorial. Explain how the number of participants needed to complete the study will vary in these examples. (270-271)

o There is an important historical connection between factorial design and agricultural research. Explain. (274-275)

Key Terms

Each of the following terms will be (a) printed in boldface in the chapter, and (b) found in the glossary at the end of the text. After you finish reading and studying the chapter, try to write definitions of each or examples that illustrate each. In parentheses after each term I've put the page on which it first appears.

Factorial design (246)

Factorial matrix (247)

Main effect (249)

Interaction (253)

Ceiling effect (257)

Mixed factorial design (262)

PxE factorial design (262)

ATI design (268)

Leakage (273)

Sample Test Items

Fill-ins

The answers to these fill-in-the-blank questions can be found in the list of key terms.

1. A _____ factorial design includes at least one between-subjects factor and at least one within-subjects factor.

2. In a factorial study, examining row means allows the experimenter to determine if a significant _____ occurred.

3. The defining feature of a _____ is the presence of two or more independent variables.

4. A _____ occurs when the means for two different conditions are very close to the maximum possible score.

5. In educational research, a(n) _____ interaction is said to occur when the effectiveness of some type of instruction depends on the type of person receiving that instruction.

6. In a _____ design, one of the factors is a manipulated variable and a second factor is a subject variable.

7. A box containing cell means for each of the conditions in a factorial study is called a _____.

8. _____ can occur in a study when participants who have completed the study confer with those about to become participants.

Matching
Terms in the left-hand column are key terms. For each term, find the correct matching example or concept description or example, and write in the letter of the term in the blank space.

A. leakage   _____ one within, one between

B. PxE factorial   _____ overall influence of one factor

C. ceiling effect   _____ 2x3, for example

D. mixed factorial _____ most dangerous when deception involved

E. ATI design   _____ scores too high for effect to be known

F. main effect   _____ effect of one IV depends on the other IV

G. interaction   _____ legacy of Kurt Lewin

H. factorial design _____ type of interaction in educational research

Multiple Choice

1. A 2x3x4 factorial design has
    a. at least one between-subjects factor
    b. nine different conditions (2 plus 3 plus 4)
    c. three different independent variables
    d. twenty-four independent variables (2 times 3 times 4)

2. In a study examining the effects of room size (large or small) and window presence (room with a window or without a window on problem solving), a researcher finds that the room size didn't affect performance, but people did a lot better when there was a window. That is, in this study,
   a. an interaction between room size and window presence occurred
   b. there was a main effect for room size only
   c. there was a main effect for window presence only
   d. there were two main effects and no interaction

3. In a 2 (gender) x 2 (type of therapy) factorial design, which of the following outcomes would be an example of an interaction?
   a. males do better in therapy A; females also do better with this therapy
   b. therapy A works better for males, while therapy B works better for females
   c. therapy B works better overall, and this is true for both males and females
   d. females outperform males, regardless of type of therapy

4. In a mixed design,
   a. there is at least one repeated measure
   b. one of the variables has to be a subject variable
   c. the number of levels for each independent variable will be different (e.g., 2x3)
   d. counterbalancing will always be needed

5. A study with at least one subject variable and one manipulated variable is referred to in the text as
   a. a PxE factorial design
   b. a mixed factorial design
   c. a nonequivalent groups factorial design
   d. an independent groups factorial design

6. Suppose you have a 2x3 factorial in which one of the factors is rat gender and the other is a repeated measure such as "trials in maze learning." Suppose cell A1B1 has 30 rats in it. How many rats will be needed for this study?
   a. 60
   b. 90
   c. 30
   d. 180

7. Consider the case studies that appeared in Chapter 8. Which of the following was a PxE factorial?
   a. the study comparing combined/noncombined images and bizarre/nonbizarre images
   b. the study of the effects of context on memory, when the lists were learned either on a beach or underwater, then recalled on one place or another
   c. the study comparing high and low self-efficacy and looming or stationary spiders
   d. the study comparing Type A and Type B people completing tasks with differing levels of difficulty

8. Which of the following was true about the famous Jenkins and Dallenbach study of retroactive interference?
   a. they showed that it was better to remain active between studying and recalling; falling asleep in between was a bad idea
   b. it was the first use of a factorial design utilizing large numbers of research participants in each group
   c. they found a main effect for retention interval but no difference for the other factor (whether or not people slept between study and recall)
   d. their results suggested an interaction – retention interval had a greater effect when the students remained awake than when they slept between study and recall

The next four questions refer to the following hypothetical study:

In a maze learning study, a researcher compares the performance of laboratory-bred white rats and wild rats that have been captured. Half the rats in each group are tested on traditional mazes with alleys (side walls); the remaining rats are tested on an "elevated" maze" – the pathways do not have walls and are elevated three feet above the floor. The main dependent variable is 'trials to criterion" – the number of trials it takes before a rat makes three consecutive errorless runs in less than three minutes.

9. How would you describe this design?
      a. it is a mixed factorial design
      b. it included both a subject variable and a manipulated variable
      c. it is a 2x2 factorial with rats randomly assigned to one of the four cells
      d. it is a nonequivalent groups factorial design

10. Suppose ten rats are tested in the alley maze. How many total rats are needed to complete the study?
      a. 10
      b. 20
      c. 40
      d. 80

11. This study lacks
      a. a repeated-measures factor
      b. a clearly defined measure of behavior
      c. any possibility of random assignment
      d. adequate sample size

12. Which of the following outcomes to this study would be an interaction?
      a. for both types of mazes, lab rats learn faster
      b. the elevated maze is learned more easily, and this is true for both wild and lab rats
      c. lab rats learn the elevated maze more easily than the alley maze, while the wild rats learn the alley maze faster
      d. all of the above, taken together, describe an interaction

Applications Exercises

8.1. Identifying Factorial Designs

For each of the following descriptions, identify the independent and dependent variables (and the measurement scale for the dependent variables), indicate the levels of the independent variables and their attributes (between- or within-subjects; manipulated or subject; if manipulated, situational, task, or instructional), and identify the type of factorial design, including the notation system (e.g., 2x3).

1. In a study of crowding, introverts and extraverts are to be compared. Some are tested in a large room (8' x 8'), others are tested in a medium-sized room (6' x 6') and others are tested in a small room (4' x 4'). To see if expectations will influence the outcome, half the participants in each group are told that the study hypothesizes that crowding will harm their performance; the remaining participants are told nothing about hypothesis being studied. While in the room, participants fill out an anxiety survey (psychological test), then listen to a series of brief segments of five heavy metal songs and rank them from the most annoying to the least annoying.

2. A cognitive psychologist interested in intelligence, expertise, and memory recruits 60 people, 30 with IQ scores between 130 and 140, and 30 with IQ scores between 100 and 110. Within each group, half could be considered experts in their knowledge of chess, while the other half would be considered beginners (i.e., know how to play, but don't play with much skill). All the participants are given five lists of words to memorize and recall.

3. To assess the effects of concurrent eating on beverage preferences, a researcher randomly assigns participants to "eating" and "non-eating" groups. Those in the first group are given a variety of snacks to eat while completing a beverage taste test; those in the second group have no snacks to eat during the taste test. In the taste test, each participant judges three varieties of wine (merlot, zinfandel, reisling). As each wine is tasted, it is judged on 5-point scales for "sweetness," "intensity," and "body." Lastly, each participant writes each of the wine's labels in an order that indicates overall preference.

4. In a study of circadian variability in skin sensitivity, a researcher examines 2-point thresholds for 20 participants. Each is tested on three different areas of the body (thumb, forehead, thigh) at three different times of the day (9 AM, 3 PM, 9 PM, and 3 AM). The 2-point threshold is the distance between two points (in cm) touching the skin, at which a participant perceives them as two points instead of one.

5. In a study of impression formation, participants see a mock interview. Half are told to think of the interview as a job interview; others are told it is a clinical interview with a criminal, to determine competency to stand trial. For each group, half see an interview in which the person being interviewed is female; remaining participants see an interview with a male being questioned. For all interviews, the person doing the interview is male. After seeing an interview, participants rate the interviewees on ten different personality variables, using 10-point scales for each.

6. In a cognitive mapping study, a researcher wants to determine if experience on campus and building usage will help students identify the locations of buildings on campus. A map of the campus is prepared that includes only the border of the school and the location of the psychology building (the experiment takes place in the psych building). Participants (freshman and sophomores, who are assumed to differ in overall familiarity with the campus) are asked to mark on the map the locations of three campus buildings that are assumed to vary in frequency of usage: the chapel (least visited), the gym (intermediate), and the dining hall (most visited). After placing each location on the map, participants indicate how confident they are of their decision (1-5 scale).

8.2. Interpreting Research with Factorial Designs

For each of the following, create the appropriate factorial matrix, calculate the row and column means, draw an accurate graph (label axes clearly), and give a good summary description of the study's results. For the purpose of the exercise, assume that row or column mean differences are significant only if they differ by at least 4.

1. A researcher is interested in the effects of rotation speed and cognitive interference on rotary pursuit performance (participants attempt to keep a stylus in contact with a small disk that is near the edge of a larger rotating disk). On some trials the speed of the rotating disk is "slow" (15 rpm) while on other trials the speed is "fast" (45 rpm). On some trials there is no cognitive interference, on others there is "low interference" (say the alphabet forward as fast as you can, skipping every other letter), and on others there is "high interference" (say the alphabet backwards as fast as you can, skipping every other letter). In a completely within-subjects procedure with proper counterbalancing, subjects participate in each of the following six conditions of this 2x3 repeated-measures factorial.

    1. slow speed (15 rpm) – no interference
    2. slow speed (15 rpm) – low interference
    3. slow speed (15 rpm) – high interference
    4. fast speed (45 rpm) – no interference
    5. fast speed (45 rpm) – low interference
    6. fast speed (45 rpm) – high interference

The researcher records the amount of time (in seconds) participants keep the stylus on the rotating disks per 20 seconds of rotation and these are the mean scores for each group:

| 1. 14 | 2. 14 | 3. 14 | 4. 12 | 5. 8 | 6. 4 |

2. A researcher is interested in how locus of control (LOC) and degree of noise predictability influence performance on a problem-solving task. On the basis of a test for LOC, the researcher identifies two groups of participants: Internals (InLOC; they generally believe they are the cause of things that happen to them) and Externals (ExLOC; they generally believe that events outside of themselves, in the environment, are the causes of things that happen to them). Participants in each group are randomly assigned to one of two conditions, Predictable Noise (PN) and Unpredictable Noise (UPN). While sitting in a room completing anagram problems (unscramble groups of letters to form words) for 15 minutes, those in the PN condition hear the sound of an airplane taking off every 45 seconds. Those in the UPN hear the same plane noises, but the planes take off at random time intervals that average to 45 seconds. Hence, there are four different conditions in this 2x2 PxE factorial design.
   1. InLOC – PN
   2. InLOC – UPN
   3. ExLOC – PN
   4. ExLOC – UPN

The researcher records the number of anagrams solved and these are the average scores for each group:

   1. 28   2. 40   3. 20   4. 12

3. A sports psychologist investigates the effects of different mental and physical strategies to see if they can improve foul shooting by players on the men's and women's basketball teams. An equal number of males and females are assigned to a control group, in which they simply practice foul shooting. In a second condition, males and females practice shooting, but they also receive training in "guided imagery," a technique designed to focus mental attention on the task. In a third condition, males and females practice shooting, receive training in guided imagery, and also receive training in progressive muscle relaxation, designed to help them reduce anxiety. The result is a 2x3 PxE design with the following six conditions:

1. males – control group
2. males – guided imagery
3. males – imagery plus relaxation
4. females – control group
5. females – guided imagery
6. females – imagery plus relaxation

To test the effectiveness of these strategies and to see if gender differences occur, all players take 60 foul shots and mean number made for each group is as follows:

1. 32   2. 43   3. 45   4. 33   5. 45   6. 45

4. A social psychologist studying obedience decides to further investigate the Milgram procedure in which teachers (the research participants) are asked to deliver shocks of increasing intensity to learners (appear to be participants but are really in the employ of the experimenter and don't really get shocked). The researcher wonders if obedience would be influenced by (a) the perceived level of prestige of the experimenter and (b) whether the apparent learner is male or female. The participants are all males, as is the experimenter. Experimenters were described either as a graduate student (low prestige) or a distinguished professor (high prestige). Hence the design is a 2x2 independent groups design with the following conditions:

   1. low experimenter prestige – female learner
   2. low experimenter prestige – male learner
   3. high experimenter prestige – female learner
   4. high experimenter prestige – male learner

The dependent variable was the number of shocks delivered by the "teacher" to the "learner." The greater the number of shocks delivered, the higher the level of obedience. The mean number of shocks per group are:

1. 8   2. 10   3. 18   4. 20

Answers to Sample Test Items

Fill-ins

1. mixed
2. main effect
3. factorial design
4. ceiling effect
5. ATI
6. PxE
7. factorial matrix
8. leakage

Matching

From top to bottom, the correct letter sequence is: D, F, H, A, C, G, B, E

Multiple Choice

1. a. not necessarily – all could be within-subjects factors
   b. there are 24 different conditions in the study (2 times 3 times 4)
   c. CORRECT ANSWER – the three IVs have 2, 3, and 4 levels, respectively
   d. there are 24 different conditions, not 24 independent variables

2. a. there is no interaction here
   b. no main effect for room size – it "didn't affect performance"
   c. CORRECT ANSWER – whether or not there was a window (regardless of room size) made a difference in their performance
   d. there was only a single main effect, for window presence

3. a. this describes a main effect for therapy type
   b. CORRECT ANSWER – the influence of one factor (therapy) depends on whether one is referring to males or females
   c. this describes a main effect for therapy type
   d. this describes a main effect for gender

4. a. CORRECT ANSWER – al mixed designs have at least one within-subjects factor (i.e., repeated measure) and one between-subjects factor
   b. true of a PxE design, but not in a mixed design
   c. not especially relevant
   d. counterbalancing might not be needed – the within-subjects factor might be "trials"

5. a. CORRECT ANSWER – the "P" (person) is the subject variable and the "E" (environment) is the manipulated factor
   b. this design includes at least one between-subjects factor and one within-subjects factor
   c. this would be true if both factors were subject variables
   d. independent groups requires random assignment, which is impossible when a subject variable is used

6. a. CORRECT ANSWER – there will be 30 males and 30 females, each getting three trials
   b. this would be true in a 2x3 mixed design if the "3" was the between-subjects factor
   c. this would be true in a 2x3 repeated-measures factorial
   d. this would be true in a 2x3 independent groups factorial design

7. a. this was an independent groups factorial
    b. this was a repeated-measures factorial
    c. this was a mixed factorial (self-efficacy will often be a subject variable, but in this particular study it was manipulated by the experimenters)
    d. CORRECT ANSWER – Type A or B was the "P" variable and task difficulty was the "E" variable

8. a. the opposite was true – staying awake produced more interference and poorer recall
    b. there were only two participants
    c. they found a big difference for the other factor
    d. CORRECT ANSWER – this was before the days of ANOVA, though, so with just two participants, conclusions about interactions cannot be made with much certainty

9. a. both factors are between-subjects variables
    b. CORRECT ANSWER – whether the rats were tame or wild is a subject variable; maze type is manipulated
    c. rats can be randomly assigned into maze type, but not into "rat type" (wild or tame)
    d. "maze type" is a manipulated factor – this is a P (rat type) x E (maze type) factorial

10. a. this would be the case in a 2x2 repeated-measures factorial with 10 subjects per cell
    b. this would be true is both types of rats learned both mazes
    c. CORRECT ANSWER – four groups, ten rats per group
    d. this would be true if there were 20 rats per group

11. a. CORRECT ANSWER – both factors are tested between subjects
    b. the learning criterion is quite clear
    c. both types of rats can be randomly assigned to maze type
    d. sample size is not mentioned in the description

12. a. this describes a main effect for rat type
    b. this describes a main effect for maze type
    c. CORRECT ANSWER – the effect of one variable (rate type) is different for each level of the other variable
    d. alternatives a. and b. describe main effects

Feedback on Applications Exercises

<u>Identifying Factorial Designs</u>

1. IV#1:   personality type (introverts, extraverts)
             between-subjects; subject variable
   IV#2:   room size (large, medium, small)
             between-subjects; manipulated variable; situational
   IV#3:   expectation (told hypothesis; not told)
             between-subjects; manipulated variable; instructional
   DVs: anxiety survey (interval); song rankings (ordinal)
   Design: 2x3x2 PxE factorial design

2. IV#1:   intelligence (high, average)
             between-subjects; subject variable
   IV#2:   chess expertise (high, low)
             between-subjects; subject variable
   DV: recall scores on the memory tests (ratio)
   Design: 2x2 nonequivalent groups factorial design

3. IV#1:   snacks present (yes, no)
             between-subjects; manipulated variable; situational
   IV#2:   variety of wine (merlot, zinfandel, reisling)
             within-subjects; manipulated variable; task
   DVs: ratings for sweetness, etc. (interval); overall preference (ordinal)
   Design: 2x3 mixed factorial design

4. IV#1:   skin location (thumb, forehead, thigh)
             within-subjects; manipulated variable; situational
   IV#2:   time of day (9 AM, 3 PM, 9 PM, and 3 AM)
             within-subjects; manipulated variable; situational
   DVs: distance perceived as two points (ratio)
   Design: 3x4 repeated-measures factorial design

5. IV#1:   type of interview expected (job, clinical)
             between-subjects; manipulated variable; instructional
   IV#2:   gender of interviewee (female, male)
             between-subjects; manipulated variable; situational
   DVs: judgments on personality factors (interval)
   Design: 2x2 independent groups factorial design

6. IV#1:   class (freshman, sophomore)
             between-subjects; subject variable
   IV#2:   campus location (chapel, gym, dining hall)
             within-subjects; manipulated variable; task
   DVs: location accuracy (ratio); confidence (interval)
   Design: 2x3 PxE mixed factorial design

Interpreting Research with Factorial Designs

1. There is a main effect rotation speed – performance is better at the slower speed (14>8). There is no main effect for degree of cognitive interference (13 is not significantly different from 11; 11 is not significantly different from 9). There is a significant interaction, however. At slow speeds, performance is the same regardless of the degree of interference(14=14=14), but at high speeds, performance deteriorates as the degree of interference increases (12>8>4).

	No interference	Low interference	High interference	*Row means*
Slow speed	14	14	14	**14**
Fast speed	12	8	4	**8**
Column means	**13**	**11**	**9**	

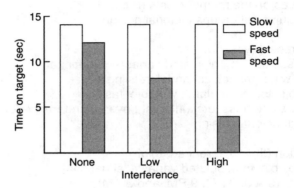

2. There is a main effect for locus of control – internals solve more anagrams than externals (34>16). There is no overall effect for level noise predictability (24 is not significantly different from 26). There is an interaction. Internals perform better with the unpredictable noise than with the predictable noise (40>28; perhaps the unpredictable noise is more of a challenge to their control), but externals perform better when the noise is predictable (20>12; they don't do well in either case, but the unpredictable noise really bothers them).

	Predictable noise (PN)	Unpredictable noise (UPN)	*Row means*
Internal LOC	28	40	**34**
External LOC	20	12	**16**
Column means	**24**	**26**	

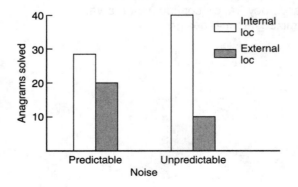

3. There are no gender differences (40 is not significantly different from 41). There is a training main effect and subsequent analysis would reveal that both imagery and imagery plus relaxation are better than no training (44>32.5 and 43.5>32.5); the relaxation training does not provide additional benefit to the imagery training, however (44 is not significantly different from 43.5). There is no significant interaction.

	Control group	Imagery group	Imagery + relaxation	Row means
Males	32	43	45	**40**
Females	33	45	45	**41**
Column means	**32.5**	**44**	**43.5**	

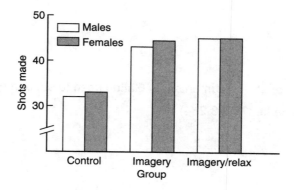

4. Obedience levels are unaffected by the gender of the learner (13 is not significantly different from 15). There is a main effect for prestige level, however – more obedience occurred when the experimenter had high prestige (19>9). There was no interaction.

	Female learner	Male learner	Row means
Low prestige	8	10	**9**
High prestige	18	20	**19**
Column means	**13**	**15**	

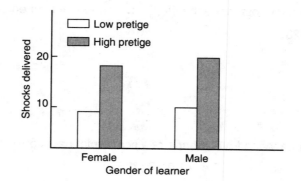

Chapter 9. Correlational Research

Reviewing the Main Concepts
After you finish reading and studying each main section of the chapter, answer the following questions to test your comprehension. The number in parentheses after each question is the page number in the text that will help you with the answer.

- *Psychology's Two Disciplines*
    - Describe the connection between Cronbach's "two disciplines" talk and the PxE factorial design that you learned about in Chapter 8. (282-283)

    - What were the arguments that Galton used to support his belief that intelligence was inherited? (283-284)

    - What was the observation made by Galton that led him to propose the concept of regression to the mean? (284)

- *Correlation and Regression – The Basics*
    - What is the difference between a positive and a negative correlation and how do the scatterplots for each differ? Give an example of each type of correlation. (286-287)

    - What happens to the shape of a scatterplot as a correlation becomes stronger (i.e., closer to +1.00 or –1.00)? (287)

o Explain why Pearson's *r* should not be used when the relationship being studied is a nonlinear one. (287-289)

o Explain why restricting the range of the scores contributing to a correlation has the effect of lowering the size of the Pearson's *r*. (289-290)

o Suppose the correlation between SAT scores and college GPA is +.40. Use the coefficient of determination to interpret the correlation. (290-291)

o What is a regression line and what is the purpose of a regression analysis? (291-293)

o In a regression analysis, what is a criterion variable and what is a predictor variable? Give examples of each. (292-293)

- *Interpreting Correlations*
  o How can the directionality problem affect the interpretation of a study that uses correlations? To illustrate the point, consider a negative correlation between anxiety and grades in school. (294)

o   Use the case study on TV and aggression to explain why a cross-lagged panel correlation can help with the directionality problem. (295-296)

o   Explain how the third variable problem can make it difficult to interpret a correlation. As an example, consider a hypothetical strong positive correlation between watching violence on TV and being aggressive. (296-297)

o   What is the purpose of calculating a partial correlation? (297-298)

o   The presence of a Pearson's r in the results doesn't necessarily mean that a correlational design has been used, and the presence of a t test or an ANOVA does not necessarily mean that a strictly experimental design has been used. Explain. (298-299)

•   *Using Correlations*
    o   On both practical and ethical grounds, a researcher sometimes has to complete a correlational study instead of an experimental study. Use an example to explain this point. (299-300)

- In psychological testing, describe how correlations can be used to establish split-half reliability. (300-301)

- Describe how correlations would be used to establish the criterion validity of a test like the K•ABC intelligence test. (301)

- Describe how a correlational design was used to test the effectiveness of cognitive therapy on depression. (301, 303)

- In his study on "the achieving society," why did McClelland study children's literature and with which other factor did he correlate the themes from that literature? How did he interpret the correlation he found? (304-305)

- How are correlations used in research designed to examine the relative contributions of heredity and environment to traits such as intelligence an shyness. (303, 305-306)

- *Multivariate Analysis*
  - What is the defining feature of a multiple regression study? (306-307)

o   Distinguish between r and R and between r^2 and R^2. (307)

o   Describe the logic of a factor analysis study. (307-308)

Key Terms

Each of the following terms will be (a) printed in boldface in the chapter, and (b) found in the glossary at the end of the text. After you finish reading and studying the chapter, try to write definitions of each or examples that illustrate each. In parentheses after each term I've put the page on which it first appears.

Positive correlation (285)

Negative correlation (285)

Pearson's r (286)

Scatterplot (286)

Restricting the range (289)

Coefficient of determination (r^2) (290)

Regression analysis (291)

Regression line (291)

Criterion variable (292)

Predictor variable (292)

Directionality problem (294)

Cross-lagged panel correlation (295)

Third variable problem (296)

Partial correlation (297)

Split-half reliability (301)

Test-retest reliability (301)

Criterion validity (301)

Bivariate (306)

Multivariate (306)

Multiple regression (306)

Factor analysis (307)

Correlation matrix (308)

Sample Test Items

Fill-ins
The answers to these fill-in-the-blank questions can be found in the list of key terms.

1. In a type of graph called a _____, the axes represent two variables being correlated.

2. In a bivariate correlation between two variables, A and B, A could be causing B or B could be causing A. This is known as the _____ problem.

3. When trying to establish the _____ of a new IQ test, a researcher would correlate the new test's scores with a score indicating achievement in school.

4. The effects of third variables can be evaluated statistically through the procedure of _____.

5. In a _____, high scores on one variable are associated with low scores on a second variable.

6. Unlike test-retest reliability, _____ reliability can be determined by administering the test just once.

7. In a _____ study, there are several predictor variables and one criterion variable.

8. On the basis of using a multivariate procedure called _____, Spearman believed that everyone possessed, to varying degrees, a general intelligence factor that he called "g."

Matching
Terms in the left-hand column are key terms. For each term, find the correct matching example or concept description or example, and write in the letter of the term in the blank space.

A. positive correlation   _____ assesses directionality

B. criterion validity   _____ amount of shared variance

C. coefficient of determination   _____ two rather than more than two

D. test-retest reliability   _____ test measures what it's supposed to measure

E. regression analysis   _____ first step in factor analysis

F. bivariate   _____ lowers Pearson's r

G. correlation matrix   _____ potential explanation for observed correlation

H. third variable   _____ high on A goes with high on B

I. restricting the range   _____ serves general goal of prediction

J. cross-lagged panel correlation   _____ indicates low measurement error

1. Which of the following correlations would be least effective for making predications?
   a. -.76
   b. +.16
   c. +1.00
   d. -.09

2. Of the following examples, which would be an example of a negative correlation?
   a. the relationship between depression and hours spent sleeping
   b. the relationship between need for achievement and GPA
   c. the relationship between grades in experimental psychology and grades in statistics
   d. the relationship between shyness and self-confidence

3. Phrenologists once believed that the strength of one's sex drive was indicated by the size of one's cerebellum. That is, there was said to be a strong positive correlation between sex drive and cerebellum size, which led to the use of cerebellum measurements as a way to gauge sex drive. What can be said about these measurements?
   a. they would be quite reliable
   b. they were a valid measure of sex drive
   c. they were neither reliable nor valid
   d. they illustrate a multivariate analysis, rather than a bivariate analysis

4. Galton discovered the principle of regression to the mean when he observed that
   a. tall parents had tall children and short parents had short children, showing that height was inherited, not the result of environmental influences
   b. parents who were much shorter than average tended to have children who were slightly taller than they were
   c. parents who were much taller than average tended to have children who were slightly taller than they were
   d. regression lines can be used for prediction purposes

5. Consider two correlations, +.50 and +.70. Which of the following is true?
   a. drawing conclusions about cause and effect is safer with the +.70 than with the +.50
   b. the points on the scatterplot would be closer to the regression line for the +.70 than for the +.50
   c. because it is "half way to being perfect," the directionality problem is more acute for the +.50 than for the +.70
   d. they could represent the exact same study, except that the +.70 would be more likely to reflect a range restriction than the +.50

6. According to the so-called Yerkes-Dodson Law, motor performance on difficult tasks is best if the person is only moderately aroused. Either high or low arousal produces poor performance. When examining the relationship between arousal and performance, which of the following is true?
   a. Pearson's r should not be used because this relationship violates the assumption of linearity
   b. this is an example of a strong positive correlation and would yield a Pearson's r somewhere in the vicinity of +.70
   c. this is an example of a strong negative correlation and would yield a Pearson's r somewhere in the vicinity of -.70
   d. because only the moderate arousal relates to good performance, there is a range restriction problem here

7. A researcher investigates exercise practices and emotional stability and finds a correlation of +.80 between a measure of exercise frequency and a measure of emotional stability (low score = unstable; high score = stable). Which of the following is true?
   a. you can safely predict that the relationship will be a strong one for 80% of the population
   b. if somebody is unstable emotionally, exercise is the cure for the problem
   c. people who exercise a lot tend to be emotionally stable
   d. emotional instability can cause somebody to drop their exercise program

8. The study by Eron and his colleagues (preference for violent TV and tendencies toward aggression) illustrated several points about the interpretation of correlational research. Which of the following was true about that study?
   a. they used a partial correlation procedure to show that the correlation between the preference for violent TV and the tendencies toward aggression disappeared when third variables were taken into account
   b. their correlations were quite low because they had a restriction of range problem
   c. by correlating preferences in the third grade with aggressive tendencies ten years later, they were able to eliminate the directionality problem
   d. they concluded that a preference for violent TV was a cause of aggression, but their study highlights the danger of saying anything about cause with a correlational study – their outcome could be the result of either the directionality problem or the third variable problem

9. To achieve criterion validity for the K•ABC test, the creators of the test
   a. gave the test twice and correlated the results
   b. correlated K•ABC scores with scores on the California Achievement Test
   c. took the K•ABC data and correlated even-numbered items with odd-numbered items
   d. correlated the "simultaneous processing" subtest scores with the subtest scores for "sequential processing"

10. On what grounds could one argue that shyness is at least partly inherited from one's parents?
   a. shy parents often have shy children
   b. there is a higher degree of similarity in shyness for identical twins than for fraternal twins
   c. there is a higher degree of similarity in shyness for identical twins reared together than for identical twins reared apart
   d. children who are shy seldom grow up to be adults who are shy

11. The procedure of combining several predictors into one, then predicting some criterion, occurs with
   a. multiple regression
   b. partial correlation
   c. factor analysis
   d. cross-lagged panel correlation

12. Which of the following was true about McClelland's famous study on the "achieving" society?
   a. he predicted societal achievement by evaluating achievement themes in children's literature
   b. he was able to show that high achievement needs in children caused later economic progress
   c. he correlated achievement scores for children and their parents
   d. he showed that the "TAT" (Thematic Apperception Test) had high reliability but questionable validity

Applications Exercises

9.1. Correlations and the Nature/Nurture Issue

As a researcher, suppose you are interested in the extent to which biological factors are associated with shyness in females. Assume you have access to 20 adopted children, all females, and you give each a shyness test. The test yields scores from 0-20 and the higher the score, the greater the degree of shyness. You also test the biological mother and the adoptive mother. Create some data and calculate the appropriate correlations that would lead you to conclude that (a) shyness is at least partially inherited, or (b) shyness seems to be primarily a function of the environment. The correlation can be calculated by following the guidelines in Appendix C of the text or by using a statistical package (e.g, SPSS).

9.2. Assessing the Effect of Outlyers

The following data were taken from a laboratory exercise I frequently use in my research methods course. Students complete one trial each of two different hand-eye coordination tests. The Purdue pegboard requires students to build a series of small objects using small washers and pegs. The Grooved Pegboard involves fitting pegs into a pegboard according to the certain orientation.

For the following data, calculate Pearson's r and create a scatterplot, either by hand or via a statistical package. Then remove the data for participant # 12 and repeat the calculations. What do you conclude?

N.B. Each of the numbers represents the time (in seconds) that it took one of my students to complete the task.

Participant	Purdue	Grooved
1	54	34
2	80	39
3	65	40
4	70	37
5	60	33
6	58	37
7	62	38
8	51	33
9	59	37
10	76	42
11	66	35
12	90	35
13	53	33
14	79	44
15	69	40
16	52	30
17	50	27

Answers to Sample Test Items

Fill-ins

    1. scatterplot
    2. directionality
    3. criterion validity
    4. partial correlation
    5. negative correlation
    6. split-half
    7. multiple regression
    8. factor analysis

Matching

    From top to bottom, the correct letter sequence is: J, C, F, B, G, I, H, A, E, D

Multiple Choice

1. a. this is a relatively strong negative correlation
    b. this is a weak correlation, but not the weakest
    c. this is the best correlation for making predictions
    d. CORRECT ANSWER – this is the correlation closest to zero

2. a. positive – greater depression is associated with more time sleeping
    b. positive – high achievement needs are likely to be associated with high achievement
    c. positive – similar skills involved
    d. CORRECT ANSWER – as shyness increases, self-confidence is likely to decrease, and
        vice-versa

3. a. CORRECT ANSWER – by measuring twice, for instance, the same basic results would
        occur
    b. Flourens showed that the cerebellum had nothing to do with sex, so the measure would
        have no validity
    c. they were reliable but not valid
    d. they illustrate a bivariate analysis (two variables – sex drive, cerebellum size)

4. a. this may be so, but it is not related to the regression to the mean phenomenon
    b. CORRECT ANSWER – these children were moving in the direction of (i.e., regressing to)
        the population mean for height
    c. these parents would have tall children, but they would be not quite as tall as the parents
    d. true, but not related to the regression to the mean phenomenon

5. a. drawing conclusions about cause an effect is not safe with either
    b. CORRECT ANSWER – as the correlation gets closer to +1.00, the points on the scatterplot
        get closer to the regression line
    c. directionality is just as likely to be a problem for each one
    d. a range restriction tends to lower the correlation, so the opposite would be true

6. a. CORRECT ANSWER – a Pearson's r would be close to zero, a misrepresentation of the
        strength of this nonlinear relationship
    b. this is strong relationship, but not a linear one
    c. this is strong relationship, but not a linear one
    d. there is no restriction problem here – levels of arousal from low to high are being measured

7. a. a Pearson's *r* has nothing to do with this type of percentage; it could be said, however, that 64% of the variability in both these factors is shared variance (+.80 squared)
   b. this implies that exercise is a cause of emotional stability, and while this could be true, this conclusion cannot be drawn from the mere presence of a correlation
   c. CORRECT ANSWER – this is simply a verbal description of the bivariate relationship
   d. this could also be true, but it's not the correct answer for the same reason that alternative b. is incorrect (correlation does mean cause)

8. a. they used a partial correlation procedure to rule out the effects of third variables
   b. restriction of range was not a problem for them
   c. CORRECT ANSWER – the aggression seen ten years *later* could not have been caused by the preferences ten years *earlier*
   d. they took steps to deal with both types of problems

9. a. this is test-retest reliability
   b. CORRECT ANSWER - the K•ABC is the predictor variable and Achievement Test is the criterion variable
   c. this is split-half reliability
   d. this correlation should be low because the two types of abilities are supposed to be distinct – a low correlation here would provide some "construct" validity for the idea of the distinction made between sequential and simultaneous processing

10. a. could be either heredity or environment
    b. CORRECT ANSWER – assuming similar rearing conditions, the only difference between the two groups is in the degree of genetic similarity
    c. this wasn't investigated in the study described in the chapter, but if it occurred, the outcome would indicate an environmental influence, not a genetic one
    d. this would support an environmental interpretation (actually the opposite is more likely to be true – shy children often become shy adults)

11. a. CORRECT ANSWER - multiple regression always has two or more predictor variables
    b. this procedure is used to statistically control for third variables
    c. this is a multivariate procedure for identifying clusters of related variables
    d. this is a bivariate procedure for dealing with the directionality problem

12. a. CORRECT ANSWER – and the achievement themes in fact predicted later economic prosperity
    b. as with other correlational research, conclusions about cause would be risky here
    c. he correlated achievement scores for children with several measures of economic health
    d. this is often concluded about the TAT, but it was not part of McClelland's research

Feedback on Applications Exercises

Correlations and the Nature/Nurture Issue

If there is an inherited side to shyness, the correlation between shyness scores for the children and the biological mothers should be higher (+.40 perhaps) than the correlation for children and the adopted mothers (+.10 perhaps). If environment is the key, the opposite should be the case.

Assessing the Effect of Outlyers

The exercise shows that one unusual score can have a noticeable effect on the size of a Pearson's r, especially when there is a relatively small amount of data. When all of the data are included, Pearson's r is +.656; when the person who trouble with the Purdue pegboard is removed, the Pearson's r drops to +.844.

Chapter 10. Quasi-Experimental Designs and Applied Research

Reviewing the Main Concepts
After you finish reading and studying each main section of the chapter, answer the following questions to test your comprehension. The numbers in parentheses after each question are the page numbers in the text that will help you with the answer.

- *Beyond the Laboratory*
  - Use the case study on the "cognitive interview" to illustrate the nature of applied research and the close relationship between basic and applied research. (318)

  - When psychology first emerged as an independent discipline at the end of the 19th century, psychologists were under pressure to show that their work could applied to benefit society. Describe two examples of how early psychologists tried to show that their work could be useful. (319-322)

  - Applied research sometimes involves a trade-off between internal and external validity. Explain. (322)

- *Quasi-Experimental Designs*
  - What is the defining feature of a study said to be "quasi-experimental?" (323)

o   What are the essential features of a nonequivalent control group design and why are they said to have a built-in confound? (323-324)

o   Explain how a selection x history problem can make it difficult to interpret what seems to be a successful outcome to a nonequivalent control group study. (324-326)

o   What is the danger of matching nonequivalent groups on pretest scores (e.g., as in the Head Start effectiveness research? (326-329)

o   In the case study on "coach effectiveness training," the researchers chose to use a nonequivalent control group design (coaches from one league got the training; coaches from another league didn't) instead of an experimental design (randomly assigning coaches from both leagues to training and no training groups). Why did they opt for the quasi-experimental design? (329-330)

o   Not all nonequivalent control group designs use pre- and posttesting. Show how the earthquake study, which didn't use pretests, still met the defining features of a nonequivalent control group design. (330-331) o What is the defining feature of an interrupted time series design? (331)

o In the case study by Wagner, a time series design evaluated the effects of a worker incentive program on productivity and the program seemed to be effective. How did Wagner address the problem of threats to the internal validity of his study? (333-334)

o What is the logic behind the use of an interrupted time series with switching replications? (334-335)

o Use the study on California's "three strikes" law to show how time series designs can be used to evaluate trends. (335)

- *Program Evaluation*
  o Use the Connecticut crackdown on speeding example (Box 10.2) to show how the use of a control comparison can make it easier to interpret the results of a time series design. (336-337)

  o In the presence of a good needs analysis, people might be "misled" into developing a new program because of the availability heuristic. Explain. (338)

o Describe five different sources of information that could contribute to a needs analysis. (338-339)

o Describe the main elements of the needs analysis completed by the Du Pont Company before they implemented a program to promote healthy behaviors in the workplace. (340)

o How does a formative evaluation differ from a summative evaluation? What is the purpose of each? (340-342)

o Program administrators and workers generally welcome formative evaluations but get quite anxious about summative evaluations. Why? (341)

o In program evaluation, a finding of "no difference" can often be an important outcome for program decision-making. Explain. (342)

o What is the essential goal of a cost-effectiveness analysis? (342-343)

o   Give two examples of how program evaluation research can utilize qualitative research? (343-344)

o   Those completing program evaluation research often face ethical dilemmas not found in traditional laboratory research. Describe three examples to illustrate the point. (344-345)

Key Terms
Each of the following terms will be (a) printed in boldface in the chapter, and (b) found in the glossary at the end of the text. After you finish reading and studying the chapter, try to write definitions of each or examples that illustrate each. In parentheses after each term I've put the page on which it first appears.

Quasi-experiment (323)

Nonequivalent control group design (323)

Regression effect (326)

Interrupted time series design (331)

Trend (331)

Interrupted time series with switching replications (334)

Program evaluation (336)

Needs analysis (338)

Key informant (339)

Focus group (339)

Community forum (339)

Formative evaluation (340)

Program audit (341)

Summative evaluation (341)

Cost-effectiveness analysis (343)

Stakeholder (345)

Sample Test Items

<u>Fill-ins</u>

The answers to these fill-in-the-blank questions can be found in the list of key terms.

1. Because multiple measurements are taken over an extended period of time, interrupted time series designs allow researchers to evaluate the influence of _____.

2. Wood and Bootzin used a(n) _____ design to evaluate the effects of an earthquake on the quantity and content of nightmares.

3. To determine if a just-completed literacy program was effective, a program evaluation researcher completed a _____.

4. Whenever participants cannot be randomly assigned to treatment conditions, the result is a _____ design.

5. If program participants are chosen in such a way that their average pretest scores are lower than the test scores for their population, their posttest scores might be higher. The program might have worked, but the outcome could also be the result of _____.

6. A agency has to decide which of two programs to implement – they appear to be equally effective. In this case the decision would probably depend on a _____.

7. As part of a formative evaluation, program evaluation researchers often conduct a

   _____.

8. Census data are most useful during the _____ stage of program evaluation.

Matching

Terms in the left-hand column are key terms. For each term, find the correct matching example or concept description or example, and write in the letter of the term in the blank space.

A. stakeholders   _____ useful for needs analysis

B. switching replication   _____ program implemented as planned?

C. focus group   _____ random assignment not possible

D. quasi-experiment   _____ posttest if pretest is an extreme score

E. trend   _____ should we create this program?

F. summative evaluation   _____ manipulated IV plus nonequivalent groups

G. regression effect   _____ includes clients, staff, and program directors

H. needs analysis   _____ evaluated in a times series study

I. program audit   _____ did the program work?

J. nonequivalent control group design   _____ program starts in different places at different times

Multiple Choice

1. Applied research is to basic research as _____ is to _____.
    a. only takes place in the field; only takes place in the lab
    b. no independent variables possible; always has independent variables
    c. no connection with theory; strong connection with theory
    d. solving specific problems; acquiring knowledge

2. Experiment is to quasi-experiment as _____ is to _____.
    a. better at external validity; better at internal validity
    b. equivalent groups; nonequivalent groups
    c. use of subject variables; use of manipulated variables
    d. control group available; no control groups used

3. Which of the following was true about the case study designed to evaluate the use of a "cognitive interview" for obtaining better eyewitness accounts?
    a. they used an interrupted time series design with a control group
    b. those trained in the technique improved, but those in the control group improved by about the same amount
    c. it was applied research, but the results provided theoretical support for the importance of context-dependent memory
    d. interview accuracy seemed to improve, but the change was probably a regression effect

4. The work of the applied psychologist Hugo Münsterberg (Box 10.1) included all of the following except
      a. applying reaction time methodology to improve the "football charging time" of linemen at Stanford
      b. identifying factors that reduced the accuracy of eyewitness memory
      c. developing and evaluating techniques for employee selection
      d. arguing that males were better suited for juries than females

5. First-year students who volunteer for a 6-month program on time management are compared with a similar group (also freshmen) who don't volunteer for the program. Their time management skills are measured before and after the program begins for the first group, using a standardized test that yields scores from 1-100 (100 = ideal time management skills). On a pretest, the volunteers score an average of 20; their posttest mean is 35. The average control group pretest score is 28 and their posttest score is 43. Which of the following is true?
      a. the changes for both groups must have been due to history
      b. the program clearly worked (assuming 35 is significantly higher than 20)
      c. there appears to be a selection x maturation problem here
      d. there is no evidence for program effectiveness

The next two questions relate to the following study: A small town decides to outlaw the use of cell phones while people are driving. Before putting the law into effect, officials measure the amount of cell phone use among drivers by placing observers at a busy intersection and recording the percentage of drivers using phones. They do this over 6 consecutive one-week intervals, each week being the middle week of a month (i.e., six months of pretesting). Right after the law is passed, officials repeat the observational study for another six months.

6. Which of the following is true about the design of this study?
      a. it is a basic interrupted time series design
      b. it is an example of a nonequivalent control group design
      c. without a control group, there is no way to evaluate trends with this design
      d. by taking multiple observations, this qualifies as a design with switching replications

7. With each number representing a percentage of drivers using cell phones during the one-week measurement intervals, which of the following sets of data would lead to the conclusion that the law reduced cell phone use, but only temporarily?
      a. 40, 35, 30, 35, 40, 35 (law goes into effect) 30, 35, 40, 35, 30, 35
      b. 40, 35, 40, 35, 40, 40 (law goes into effect) 35, 30, 25, 25, 20, 25
      c. 35, 35, 40, 35, 30, 25 (law goes into effect) 20, 15, 10, 10, 10, 10
      d. 40, 40, 35, 35, 40, 35 (law goes into effect) 25, 20, 20, 30, 40, 40

8. Nonequivalent control groups usually include pretests, but this is not necessarily the case. Which of the following studies did not include any pretesting and why?
      a. the study of the effects of the earthquake on dreams; doing a pretest would have required an accurate earthquake prediction
      b. the study on coaches effectiveness training; doing a pretest would have given away the purpose of the study
      c. the Connecticut speeding study; a pretest wasn't possible because it was a field study
      d. the study evaluating the effectiveness of Head Start; doing a pretest would have caused a regression problem

9. Consulting with "key informants" is most likely to occur during which type of program evaluation?
      a. cost analysis
      b. summative analysis
      c. formative analysis
      d. needs analysis

10. What is the advantage of doing a formative evaluation?
    a. it enables the agency to decide whether or not to implement the program
    b. it allows program changes to be made before it is too late
    c. it allows the researcher to complete an experimental study instead of a quasi-experimental study
    d. it allows for a final "formed" evaluation of the success or failure of the program

11. A cost-effectiveness analysis answers which of the following questions?
    a. Is this program running as it was designed to run?
    b. Did the program produce significant results?
    c. Should we continue with program A or program B?
    d. Does the community desire this program?

12. Sometimes the result of a program evaluation study is a "failure to reject H_0." Which of the following is true about this outcome?
    a. the outcome tells you that the program being tested was a failure
    b. the outcome doesn't allow you to conclude anything about the program
    c. the outcome can provide useful information for decisions about program effectiveness
    d. the outcome is sure to be a Type I error

Applications Exercise

10.1. Evaluating Quasi-Experimental Designs

For each of the following descriptions of quasi-experiments, construct a graph from the data and then evaluate the conclusion drawn by the researcher. That is, determine whether the conclusion is justified by the results or if an alternative explanation for the outcome is possible. Also, identify any methodological problems that ought to be corrected.

1. To test the effectiveness of an employee incentive plan on employee morale, a program evaluator used a nonequivalent control group design in a company that manufactured electric trains. The incentive plan created five-person work groups that set productivity goals, and bonuses occurred when the groups met certain goals. The unit that was given the incentive program was made up of workers who had been with the company for at least 10 years (and therefore familiar with company operations). The control group was a unit that was randomly selected from other units in the organization. Before and after the plan was implemented, productivity (number of trains produced per day) was measured. The evaluator pronounced the program a success after these results occurred:
   program group pretest = 45
   program group posttest = 53
   control group pretest = 38
   control group posttest = 46

2. To evaluate the effect of special program to improve the spelling of second graders weak in spelling, a researcher completed a nonequivalent control group design. On the basis of teacher recommendations, 20 students known to be poor spellers were identified and placed in an experimental group. Another 20 students were randomly selected from second grade classes and placed in a control group. The pretest and posttest measures of spelling ability were lists of 40 spoken words that had to be written down by the students. After getting these results, the researcher recommended implementing the spelling program for all poor spelling second graders statewide:
   pretest spelling program group: 18
   posttest spelling program group: 24
   pretest control group: 35
   posttest control group: 36

3. Alarmed at the large number of children being injured in car crashes during the first six months of 1997, state X debates a tough child restraint law during the fall of 1997. The law passes and goes into effect on January 1 of 1998. Injury rates are recorded every six months (January and June for the prior six months). Several years later, a time series analysis evaluates the effect of the new law – the dependent variable is the number of children aged 1-10 per thousand injured in car accidents. On the basis of the following data, the researcher concludes that the program did not have a significant effect:

January 1996	269	January 1998	293
June 1996	239	June 1998	217
January 1997	280	January 1999	225
June 1997	358	June 1999	212

4. In an effort to improve the driving performance of its home delivery pizza drivers, a pizza chain with stores in Illinois, Indiana, and Ohio decides to implement a safety training program, with incentives to encourage safe driving. The training program occurs for the Indiana stores in December and for the Ohio stores the following May (Ohio is a switching replication). The Illinois stores serve as a control group. Unknown to drivers, a "safety" score is calculated for each driver once a month; it is a combination scores based on unobtrusive observations of their seat belt use and their speed 100 yards away from the store. A low score is good and a high score is bad. The company concludes that the training program is a success, based on the following overall scores for drivers in each state (scores recorded every month, beginning six months prior to the first training program in Indiana):

Indiana: 41, 46, 39, 38, 38, 41, 39, 22, 28, 25, 29, 35, 41, 40, 32, 33, 28, 28
Illinois: 45, 43, 41, 43, 40, 38, 37, 26, 27, 29, 31, 33, 39, 33, 39, 37, 29, 31
Ohio: 30, 31, 29, 32, 31, 24, 18, 10, 10, 11, 13, 20, 13, 10, 07, 07, 10, 08

Answers to Sample Test Items

Fill-ins

1. trends
2. nonequivalent control group
3. summative evaluation
4. quasi-experimental
5. regression
6. cost-effectiveness analysis
7. program audit
8. needs analysis

Matching

From top to bottom, the correct letter sequence is: C, I, D, G, H, J, A, E, F, B

Multiple Choice

1. a. some applied research occurs in labs and some basic research occurs in the field
   b. independent variables are common in applied research and not all basic research
      manipulates independent variables (e.g., correlational research)
   c. both basic and applied research can be theory-based
   d. CORRECT ANSWER – applied research tends to be more immediately useful than
      basic research

2. a. if anything, the reverse might be true
   b. CORRECT ANSWER – the experiment can randomly assign, the quasi-experiment cannot
   c. the reverse would be true
   d. control groups may or may not be used in both types

3. a. they used nonequivalent control group design
   b. those in the control group did not improve significantly
   c. CORRECT ANSWER – the study shows how applied research, even though it is aimed
      at a specific problem, can still contribute to our general knowledge about some
      phenomenon (memory)
   d. interview accuracy improved for those trained, and there was no evidence of a
      regression effect

4. a. CORRECT ANSWER - this example of applied research was done by Walter Miles
      and the apparatus is pictured in Figure 10.2
   b. this was part of Münsterberg's contribution to forensic psychology
   c. this was part of Münsterberg's contribution to industrial psychology
   d. this was a controversial part of Münsterberg's contribution to forensic psychology

5. a. maturation is a much more likely determinant of the increase in both groups (as
      freshmen gain experience in college, their time management skills improve)
   b. the fact that the control group increased by the same amount calls this conclusion into
      question
   c. this could only occur if one group improved (through maturation) while the other group
      didn't improve (but both improved)
   d. CORRECT ANSWER- and this is why it's nice to have a control group

6. a. CORRECT ANSWER – this is an interrupted time series without a control group
   b. there's no control group and there are multiple measuring points before and after the program goes into effect
   c. the reason for the multiple measuring points before and after the program is to enable the evaluate of a trend without necessarily using a control group
   d. multiple observations makes it a time series, duplicating the program in another place at another time constitutes "switching replications"

7. a. this is a cyclical trend
   b. even though the percentages afterwards are relatively high, this outcome still suggests that the law produced a reliable drop in cell phone use
   c. this suggests a general trend toward decreased cell phone use that began four months before the law went into effect
   d. CORRECT ANSWER – there is an initial decline, but then cell phone use begins to increase

8. a. CORRECT ANSWER – students in earthquake and no earthquake locations were the nonequivalent groups; pretest measures would have required knowing when the earthquake was going to occur
   b. a pretest of self esteem was used in this study
   c. this was a time series, not a nonequivalent control group design
   d. forcing nonequivalent groups to be equal by matching on a pretest can cause a regression effect

9. a. true only if your key informant happens to be a cost accountant
   b. a statistician or research design expert might be used as a consultant here
   c. someone with expertise in qualitative analysis might be useful as a consultant here
   d. CORRECT ANSWER – knowledgeable community leaders often have a strong sense of what types of programs might be needed in a community

10. a. this happens in a needs analysis
    b. CORRECT ANSWER – this would be a potential benefit of doing the program monitoring that happens with a formative evaluation
    c. it is highly unlikely that a formative evaluation will be using the experimental method
    d. this happens in a summative evaluation

11. a. this is a formative evaluation question
    b. this is a formative summative question
    c. CORRECT ANSWER – two programs that are about equal in effectiveness might differ in cost, and cost would determine which program is chosen
    d. this is a needs analysis question

12. a. not necessarily - the outcome might tell you that a new program just as effective as a program given to the control group
    b. the conclusion would have to be tentative, but it could be a potentially important result (as in the feedback for alternative c.)
    c. CORRECT ANSWER – it might indicate that an expensive new program doesn't work any better than the traditional program (the result would need replication though)
    d. a Type I error can only occur when H_0 is rejected

Feedback on Applications Exercise

<u>Evaluating Quasi-Experimental Designs</u>

1. There are two problems with the conclusion drawn. First, although productivity did increase for the program group, it also increased for the control group, and by the same amount. Thus, whatever might have produced the increase for the control group could also have produced the increase for the program group. For example, perhaps all of the productivity numbers are relatively low and the changes in both cases are the result of regression. Perhaps some event (i.e., history) intervened between pre- and posttest and the result was an increase in productivity. Second, the professed purpose of the study was to see if the program would improve morale, yet the behavior measured was productivity, which may or may not be related to morale – that is, the researcher used the wrong dependent variable.

Concerning the design of the study, there doesn't seem to be good justification for selecting veteran workers for the program group. It would have been better to try to reduce the nonequivalence of the groups by picking groups that were similar in terms of levels of experience.

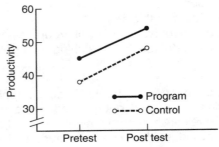

2. The program group certainly showed an increase in spelling performance, while the control group showed no improvement. There are problems of interpretation, however, making it impossible to conclude with any certainty that "the program improved spelling." Because the pretest score is so low in the program group, their apparent improvement could be a regression effect, at least in part. Second, it is likely that the results for the control group reflect a ceiling effect – their pretest score was so high that significant improvement was virtually impossible. Thus, to say that the control group showed "no improvement" distorts the true outcome.

Concerning the design of the study, this is a case in which an experimental design might be feasible – randomly assign poor spellers to a program group and a waiting list control group. If a nonequivalent control group design must be used, it would have been better to screen out really good spellers in the control group and try to populate the control group with "average" spellers. An ideal nonequivalent control group design would compare two groups of poor spellers, perhaps from two similar school districts.

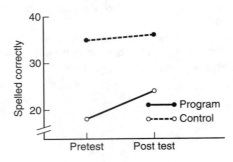

3. The researcher probably suspects a regression effect and that certainly seems to be operating to some extent here. Note the decline from June of 97 to January of 98—it happened before the law actually went into effect. The continuing decline for the following six months could also be partly due to regression, but it is possible that a true program effects occurred as well. Statistical analysis would have to confirm it, but it looks like the last three data points are reliably lower than the first three points.

Concerning the design of the study, comparisons with a similar state might help to separate program effects from regression effects.

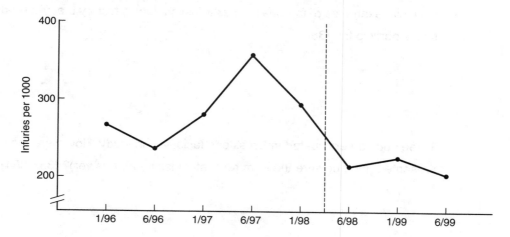

4. It isn't clear if this program is a success or not. Performance improvemes after the program is put into effect in Indiana in December, but there is a similar dip for Illinois, the control state. It is likely that some kind of seasonal trend exists, with scores being lower in the winter months. Perhaps the winter weather forces more careful driving. Scores increase (and driving performance deteriorates) as the weather improves in both states, further evidence of a seasonal trend. On the other hand, performance improves even in the summer for the replication state of Ohio. Ohio shows the same seasonal trend as Indiana and Illinois, but the improvement after program implementation cannot be a seasonal trend. The fact that driving is better in general for Ohio pizza drivers suggests a subject selection effect is operating. Maybe the Ohio drivers, better to begin with, were more open to further training.

Concerning the design of the study, it might have been better to implement the training programs for the two experimental groups closer together in time (e.g., May for one, July for another). That way the immediate post-program tests would occur during similar weather.

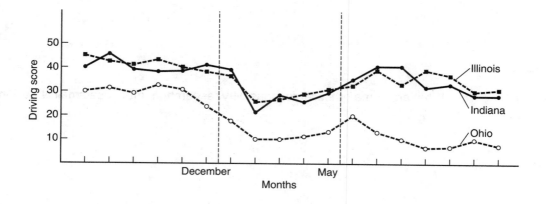

Chapter 11. Small N Designs

Reviewing the Main Concepts
After you finish reading and studying each main section of the chapter, answer the following questions to test your comprehension. The numbers in parentheses after each question are the page numbers in the text that will help you with the answer.

- *Research in Psychology Began with Small N*
    - o Give two examples of famous studies in psychology's history that featured a single participant. (352)

    - o Three people participated in Dressler's facial vision study. How were their data presented (hint: be sure the term replication is in your answer)? (353-354)

    - o Part two of Dressler's study showed good falsification thinking. Explain. (353)

- *Reasons for Small N Designs*
    - o Use the concept-learning example to illustrate how grouping data can suggest a conclusion that is not warranted by the behavior of individual participants. (357-359)

    - o What are some practical reasons why researchers often use small N designs? (359-360)

- *The Experimental Analysis of Behavior*
  - o Describe B. F. Skinner's attitude about sample size and show how he was influenced by Pavlov's thinking. (360)

  - o What was Skinner's preferred dependent variable and why did he prefer it? (360)

  - o According to Skinner's experimental analysis of behavior, what three things are needed to be able to predict and control behavior? (361)

  - o Skinner favored an inductive approach to science. Explain. (363)

  - o Consider the case study on schedules of reinforcement. In what sense is it methodologically identical to Dressler's facial vision study? (364-365)

  - o Distinguish between the contemplative ideal and the technological ideal. Give an example to show which of these ideals best fits Skinner. (365-366)

- o Explain why Skinner's goal of "control" is such a controversial issue. (366-367)

- **Small N Designs in Applied Behavior Analysis**
    - o What three elements characterize all single-subject designs? (368-369)

    - o What is the essential logic underlying the use of a withdrawal design? (369)

    - o Why is an A-B-A-B design an improvement over an A-B-A design? (369)

    - o Under what circumstances is a multiple baseline design preferred over a withdrawal design? (370-371)

    - o Describe the three varieties of multiple baseline design. (371)

    - o The case study on stuttering, using a multiple baseline design, responds to two criticisms frequently made about single-subject designs. Explain. (372-374)

- Describe the logic of a changing criterion design and relate it to the operant concept of shaping. (374-375)

- Use the case study using a changing criterion design to illustrate what is meant by the concept of social validity. (376-377)

- What purposes are served by the following designs: A-B-C-B, A–A$_1$–B–A$_1$–B, alternating treatments? (377-378)

- Excluding the points made with reference to the case study on stuttering, describe the criticisms that have been made of small N designs in the operant tradition. (378-379)

- *Psychophysics*
  - Using a hearing test as a example, describe Fechner's three methods of psychophysics. (380-381)

  - Why is psychophysics research considered an example of small N research? (381-382)

Key Terms

Each of the following terms will be (a) printed in boldface in the chapter, and (b) found in the glossary at the end of the text. After you finish reading and studying the chapter, try to write definitions of each or examples that illustrate each. In parentheses after each term I've put the page on which it first appears.

Individual-subject validity (357)

Operant conditioning (360)

Rate of response (360)

Cumulative recorder (361)

Applied behavior analysis (367)

Baseline (368)

A-B design (369)

Withdrawal design (369)

A-B-A design (369)

A-B-A-B design (369)

Multiple baseline design (371)

Changing criterion design (374)

Shaping (374)

Social validity (376)

A-B-C-B design (377)

$A-A_1-B-A_1-B$ design (378)

Alternating treatments design (378)

Psychophysics (380)

Absolute threshold (380)

Difference threshold (380)

Method of limits (380)

Method of constant stimuli (381)

Method of adjustment (381)

Sample Test Items

Fill-ins

The answers to these fill-in-the-blank questions can be found in the list of key terms.

1. In a Skinnerian experimental analysis of behavior, the only valuable dependent variable is _____.

2. In terms of its ability to rule out alternative explanations for a behavior change, the _____ design is the weakest of the single-subject designs.

3. The first step in any applied behavior analysis is to establish a _____ level of responding.

4. The single-subject procedures of A-B-A and A-B-A-B are both examples of _____ designs.

5. The _____ design is based on the operant procedure called shaping.

6. A researcher wishes to examine the effects of a reinforcement program on a child's behavior, as it occurs in three different environments. A _____ design should be used to evaluate the program.

7. A comparison between contingent and noncontingent reinforcement can be made by using a _____ design.

8. When using the psychophysics method of _____, participants make judgments about a series of stimuli that vary in intensity and are presented in a random order.

Matching

Terms in the left-hand column are key terms. For each term, find the correct matching example or concept description or example, and write in the letter of the term in the blank space.

A. A-B   _____ value of program recognized by participants?

B. cumulative recorder   _____ stacked graphs

C. individual-subject validity   _____ alternating trials – ascend, descend

D. multiple baseline   _____ best approach for improving physical health

E. method of limits   _____ treatment evaluated twice

F. changing criterion   _____ its weakness led to withdrawal designs

G. A-B-A-B   _____ does grouped data reflect individuals?

H. operant conditioning   _____ could evaluate two therapies at once

I. alternating treatment   _____ visual image of rate of response

J. social validity   _____ a matter of consequences

Multiple Choice

1. In psychology's early years, approximately 1880-1920,
   a. most research was purely qualitative, because statistical analysis didn't develop until the 1930s (with Fisher and ANOVA)
   b. a typical study involves 2-3 participants, with complete data for each person described
   c. most research involved the study of animals (e.g., maze learning)
   d. most research summarized data from relatively large samples, but only descriptive statistics were used (e.g., means, graphs)

2. Which of the following is true about Thorndike's research on cats in puzzle boxes?
   a. it failed the individual-subject validity test
   b. it shows the limitations of studying just a single cat – no external validity
   c. it is an example of an unfortunate tendency among early researchers to attribute human characteristics to animals – it failed the parsimony test
   d. it illustrates the strategy of using additional subjects for the purpose of replication

3. Which of the following is true about "continuity theory" in the concept-learning area?
   a. it is a reasonably good explanation of the gradual process of trial and error learning that occurs when children learn concepts
   b. it shows how faulty conclusions can result when grouped data does not reflect individual performance
   c. it has been replaced by a theory that blends continuity and noncontinuity
   d. it shows how a theory can hold up over time, even if it is based on small N research

4. Compared to an A-B-A design, an A-B-A-B design
   a. includes a withdrawal procedure
   b. is less parsimonious and is therefore less likely to be used
   c. tests treatment effectiveness more frequently
   d. includes two periods in which treatment does not occur

5. Skinner would agree with all of the following statements except
   a. operant workers should focus on doing the basic research to understand the experimental analysis of behavior – applications can wait
   b. if you adequately control conditions, you will observe orderly behavior
   c. in an experimental analysis of behavior, the only result worth recording is whether or not a behavior occurs and how often it occurs
   d. behavior is controlled by the consequences that immediately follow the behavior

6. So-called single-subject designs include all of the following elements except
   a. a stage during which treatment is withdrawn
   b. clear operational definitions of the behavior(s) to be changed
   c. establishing a baseline level of responding
   d. introducing some treatment program after a baseline has been established

7. The example of training asthmatic children to use a breathing device illustrated which design?
   a. multiple baseline
   b. A-B-C-B
   c. changing criterion
   d. withdrawal

8. Consider the case study that used a multiple baseline design to evaluate a program to improve the speaking behavior of children with stuttering problems. Which of the following is true about that study?
   a. it illustrated the kind of multiple baseline in which the same behavior is changed in a single individual in several environments (e.g., home and school)
   b. multiple baselines were established with "multiple children" (i.e., program introduced at different times for different children)
   c. it illustrates a problem with some single-subject research – a lack of follow-up data
   d. the stuttering returned when the program was withdrawn

9. The case study by Hume and Crossman was designed to evaluate a program to improve the out-of-pool practice time of adolescent boys on a swim team. Which of the following was true about the study?
   a. it compared 2 types of reinforcement contingencies, thereby using an A-B-C-B design
   b. it used an A-B-A design
   c. it established multiple baselines, one for each swimmer
   d. productive behaviors increased both times the treatment was introduced

10. Social validity is said to exist when
    a. the results generalize to other social environments
    b. the results for the group as a whole reflect individual behavior
    c. a successful program is actually used by people
    d. the results for one person are replicated with other people

11. In an A-A_1-B-A_1-B single-subject design
    a. A and A_1 refer to drug and placebo, respectively
    b. A and A_1 are two different persons
    c. A and A_1 refer to contingent and noncontingent reinforcement
    d. A and A_1 refer to two separate baselines

12. On a hearing test, Ed hears tones that get progressively softer and he is told to press a button if he hears the sound. Ed is experiencing
    a. the psychophysics method of gradual adjustment
    b. the method of constant stimuli
    c. descending trials of the method of limits
    d. a test for difference thresholds

Applications Exercise

11.1. Outcomes of Single-Subject Designs

For each of the following descriptions of studies, prepare a graph from the data to illustrate each of the outcomes, and write a conclusion.

1. An applied behavior analyst wishes to determine if an antianxiety drug will help a person with a mild social phobia interact with strangers in a group therapy situation. The client wears a heart rate monitor and the researcher records heart rate every ten minutes (assume that anxiety increases heart rate) during five consecutive 50-minute group therapy situations. Using an A-A_1-B-A_1-B design, the following results occur:

   A :   93, 98, 88, 95, 91
   A_1 :   78, 83, 85, 77, 73
   B :   70, 66, 59, 62, 63
   A_1 :   69, 77, 72, 74, 80
   B :   66, 58, 55, 61, 59

2. Using an A-B-C-B design, an applied behavior analyst wishes to determine if the bed-making behavior of a moderately retarded 8-year old boy can be improved. On "contingent" days, the boy is given 10 tokens (can be later turned in for more concrete rewards) immediately after successfully making his bed. On "noncontingent" days, he is given the tokens at lunchtime, assuming that he successfully made his bed that morning. For the following data, each number represents the number of times the boy makes his bed over a 10-day interval.

   A :   2, 1, 3, 2
   B :   5, 9, 8, 10
   C :   4, 3, 5, 4
   B :   9, 8, 9, 10

3. To enhance levels of concentration during foul-shooting drills, a behavior analytically inclined basketball coach starts an incentive program. Three players are told they can accumulate points for successful foul-shooting and a certain number of points will get them out of practice early. Using a multiple baseline design (one behavior, one environment, three participants), the numbers recorded are the number of made free throws out of a set of 20. These results occur (n.b. underlined numbers are baseline data):

Player #1: 08, 09, 11, 10, 13, 17, 18, 18, 19, 17, 20, 18, 18
Player #2: 07, 07, 10, 12, 14, 13, 14, 15, 17, 18, 19, 20, 19
Player #3 03, 01, 04, 07, 05, 09, 03, 02, 06, 02, 03, 05, 04

4. A behavior analyst decides to use an A-B-A-B design to evaluate a program to increase seat belt use. During the treatment phase of the program, seat belt reminder signs are placed around an employee parking lot. Observers then record seat belt use among drivers exiting from the lot. Each phase of the A-B-A-B design lasts for a workweek (Monday through Friday) and each data point represents the percentage of drivers using seatbelts on any given day.

A :   45, 56, 51, 44, 55
B :   56, 53, 71, 78, 82
A :   66, 55, 53, 59, 63
B :   75, 88, 82, 91, 84

Answers to Sample Test Items

<u>Fill-ins</u>
1. rate of response
2. A-B
3. baseline
4. withdrawal
5. changing criterion
6. multiple baseline
7. A-B-C-B
8. constant stimuli

<u>Matching</u>

From top to bottom, the correct letter sequence is: J, D, E, F, G, A, C, I, B, H

<u>Multiple Choice</u>

1. a. true about Fisher, but even before ANOVA, much research was quantitative
   b. CORRECT ANSWER – with the Dressler study on facial vision as a prime example
   c. most research involved human participants ("observers")
   d. some research summarized data from relatively large samples, but most research involved small N

2. a. this can only occur if data from large groups is combined and the group averages don't reflect individual behavior – Thorndike didn't combine the data
   b. Thorndike replicated his results on a number of cats
   c. Thorndike did the opposite – his explanation was quite parsimonious
   d. CORRECT ANSWER – Thorndike tested several cats and presented data for each

3. a. noncontinuity theory provides a better explanation
   b. CORRECT ANSWER – grouping the data disguised the hypothesis-testing strategies used by children
   c. it has been replaced by noncontinuity theory
   d. it was based on large N research and it hasn't held up over time

4. a. this is true of both designs (when "A" follows "B")
   b. because it evaluates the program twice, it is more likely to be used
   c. CORRECT ANSWER – treatment = "B"
   d. this is true of both designs (signified by "A")

5. a. CORRECT ANSWER – Skinner was a strong advocate of application, so he would disagree with this statement
   b. he would agree – this paraphrases Pavlov, one of Skinner's idols
   c. he would agree – this is a reference to the reliance on response as the preferred dependent variable
   d. he would agree – this is the cornerstone of operant conditioning

6. a. CORRECT ANSWER – not all designs have a withdrawal stage (e.g., multiple baseline)
   b. precise definitions are essential
   c. establishing baseline is always the first step
   d. all single-subject designs essentially start with A-B

7. a. CORRECT ANSWER – and it was the type of multiple baseline in which several behaviors are changed for a single individual
   b. this design compares contingent vs. noncontingent reinforcement
   c. this design compares different programs
   d. this design introduces a treatment program then removes it

8. a. the program was introduced in one environment – the home; data were collected at school, however, as a way of testing generalization
   b. CORRECT ANSWER – there were eight different children in the study
   c. lack of follow-up is sometimes used as a criticism of this type of research, but this study included follow-up data, strengthening the conclusion about program success
   d. this is a good example of a situation in which a withdrawal design might be rejected on ethical grounds (once a child stops stuttering, why take the chance of having the behavior return by removing the program?)

9. a. it compared examined contingent vs. noncontingent reinforcement, but did not use the A-B-C-B design
   b. it used an A-B-A-B design
   c. it did not use a multiple baselines design
   d. CORRECT ANSWER - productive behaviors increased both times when the "B" followed the "A" in this A-B-A-B design

10. a. this is external validity
    b. this is individual-subject validity
    c. CORRECT ANSWER – social validity also involves whether the program has value for improving society and whether its value is perceived as such by the study's participants
    d. this is simply the replication issue

11. a. CORRECT ANSWER – this design is often used to evaluate drug effectiveness
    b. evaluating two different persons probably requires a multiple baseline design
    c. contingent and noncontingent reinforcement are evaluated in an A-B-C-B design
    d. this is not a multiple baseline design

12. a. in the method of adjustment, Ed would be controlling volume himself
    b. in the method of constant stimuli, the stimuli would appear in random sequences of loudness
    c. CORRECT ANSWER – the tones begin above the threshold for hearing, then gradually descend until they can no longer be heard
    d. this is a test for an absolute threshold (the point distinguishing hearing from not hearing a tone)

Feedback on Applications Exercise

<u>Outcomes of Single-Subject Designs</u>

1. Compared to baseline heart rate levels (A), there appears to be a reliable reduction when the placebo has been administered (A_1). However, the heart rate goes down even further when the actual antianxiety drug is used (B). In this study, then, there is both a placebo effect and a true drug effect operating.

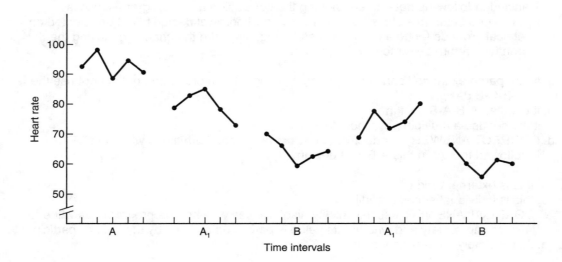

2. The contingent reinforcement (B) clearly has the effect of producing a high rate of bed-making behavior. However, the noncontingent reinforcement (C) also seems to have a small effect, at least compared to baseline (A). Perhaps the presence of *any* reinforcement produces a positive attitude in the boy and that positive feeling manifests itself in a slight increase in bed making.

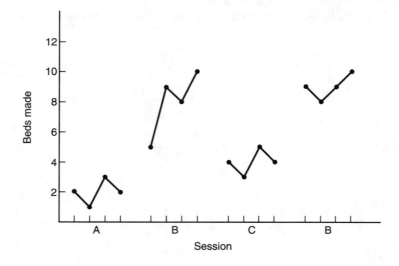

3. The coach needs to try something else. It looks like the program might have worked for player #1, although a general improvement with time cannot be ruled out. Improvement with time clearly seems to be happening with player #2. Not much of anything seems to be happening with player #3, who just seems to be an incompetent and/or uninterested foul shooter.

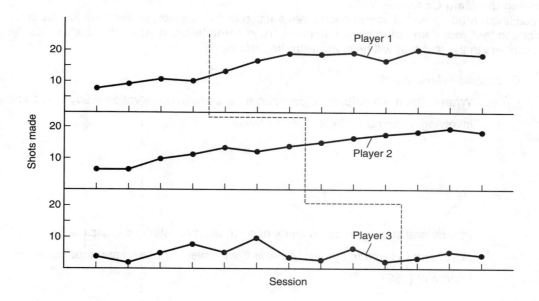

4. The program appears to be effective. Seat belt use increases when the signs first appear (although it evidently takes a few days for drivers to notice them), usage drops again when the signs are removed, then increases again when the signs reappear. Usage in the withdrawal phase appears to be slightly higher than the original baseline, suggesting that some drivers began using their seatbelts after the initial treatment period, and continuing to buckle up thereafter.

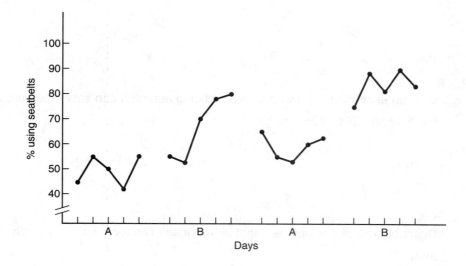

Chapter 12. Descriptive Research Methods

Reviewing the Main Concepts
After you finish reading and studying each main section of the chapter, answer the following questions to test your comprehension. The numbers in parentheses after each question are the page numbers in the text that will help you with the answer.

- *Observational Research*
  - What is the main difference between a naturalistic observation study and a study involving participant observation? (389)

  - In a naturalistic observation study of animals, it is usually impossible for observers to remain "hidden." How is the problem of observer unobtrusiveness handled? (389)

  - What was (a) a methodological problem and (b) an ethical dilemma faced by Festinger in is famous participant observation study? (390-391)

  - Give an example to show how observational research can serve the purpose of falsification. (391-392)

  - Describe how observer bias might be reduced in observational research. (392-393) o What is meant by reactivity and how do researchers try to eliminate it in observational research? (393-394)

o Why is it sometimes difficult to meet the requirements of the APA ethics code when doing certain types of observational research? (394)

o Use the case study on touching to illustrate the concepts of time sampling and event sampling. (396)

o Use the case study on altruism to explain why researchers sometimes impose structure by creating situations to be observed. (397-398)

- *Survey Research*
    o Describe the advantages and disadvantages of using face-to-face interviews as a survey method. (398-399)

    o Give examples to illustrate the difference between an open-ended question and a closed question on a written survey. (399)

- What can be done to increase the chances that respondents will fill out a written survey and return it? (400)

- What are the advantages and disadvantages of phone surveying? (400-401)

- How can a social desirability bias influence the results of survey research? (401-402)

- The ethics box describes a situation in which a journalist was fired based on survey data. Why was this an ethical issue? (403-404)

- *Case Studies*
  - Give examples to describe two different varieties of case study research. (405-406)

  - What are the problems associated with case study research and how can this method yield valuable information? (409-410)

- *Archival Research*
  - o What is the defining feature of archival research? (410-411)

  - o What are the strengths and weaknesses of archival research? (413-414)

Key Terms
Each of the following terms will be (a) printed in boldface in the chapter, and (b) found in the glossary at the end of the text. After you finish reading and studying the chapter, try to write definitions of each or examples that illustrate each. In parentheses after each term I've put the page on which it first appears.

Naturalistic observation (389)

Participant observation (389)

Observer bias (392)

Behavior checklist (393)

Interobserver reliability (393)

Time sampling (393)

Event sampling (393)

Reactivity (393)

Unobtrusive measures (394)

Survey (398)

Representative sample (398)

Interview survey (398)

Written survey (399)

Open-ended questions (399)

Closed questions (399)

Nonresponse bias (400)

Phone surveying (401)

Social desirability bias (401)

Sample frame (404)

Case study (405)

Archival research (410)

Content analysis (411)

Sample Test Items

<u>Fill-ins</u>

The answers to these fill-in-the-blank questions can be found in the list of key terms.

1. In the method of _____, the researcher becomes a member of the group being observed.

2. In observational research, the observer's presence might cause _____ in participants.

3. If an observational study uses just a single observer, then _____ cannot be calculated.

4. Freud's preferred method for collecting data was the _____ method.

5. Phone surveys should be brief; hence, they should rely more on _____ questions than on _____ questions.

6. In _____ research, the investigator examines data that has already been accumulated for some other purpose.

7. On a survey, respondents with a _____ bias will respond the way they think they are supposed to respond, rather than as a reflection of their true beliefs or feelings.

8. An example of an _____ would be to record the number of fingerprints on the glass cases of different exhibits in a museum.

Matching

Terms in the left-hand column are key terms. For each term, find the correct matching example or concept description or example, and write in the letter of the term in the blank space.

A. archival research	_____	the mind of a mnemonist
B. closed question	_____	designed to reduce observer biasing effects
C. content analysis	_____	responders very different from nonresponders
D. time sampling	_____	informed consent normally waived
E. nonresponse bias	_____	organize qualitative information into categories
F. sample frame	_____	record behavior at specific intervals
G. case study	_____	no reactivity problems here
H. naturalistic observation	_____	list of those who could be in a survey
I. behavior checklist	_____	Kinsey's research on sex for example
J. interview survey	_____	yes or no is the response

Multiple Choice

1. In naturalistic observational studies with animals, how is the problem of subject reactivity handled?
   a. observers simply make sure they are hidden from the animals
   b. observers assume that the animals will eventually habituate to their presence
   c. observers rely on video recordings only
   d. none of the above – reactivity only occurs with human participants

2. Hall and Veccia's study on male-female patterns of touching included
    a. interviews with couples
    b. naturalistic observation with no structure imposed by researchers
    c. participant observation with informed consent
    d. observations occurring in a structured environment created by the researchers

3. Which of the following characterized Festinger's observational research on religious cults?
    a. the presence of Festinger's participant observers might have strengthened the commitment levels of cult members
    b. as in virtually all participant research, even today, informed consent of group being observed was not obtained
    c. Festinger's observers carried hidden tape recorders, making it easy to accumulate data without relying on memory
    d. Festinger was able to show how cults broke apart after a prophecy failed

4. Observer bias
    a. is more likely to occur in naturalistic observation than in participant observation
    b. can be eliminated by using unobtrusive measures of behavior
    c. is the reason why observational research cannot be used for falsification purposes
    d. can be reduced by using behavior checklists

5. Compared to other surveying techniques, which of the following is true about face-to-face interviews?
    a. the researcher is more likely to be confined to closed questions
    b. question ambiguity is more of a problem
    c. cross-race bias is more likely to occur
    d. sampling is less of a problem

6. There are several ways to increase the return rate of a mailed written survey. Which of the following is not one of them?
    a. include more open-ended questions than closed questions (shows respondents that you really care about their opinions)
    b. send a reminder after a certain period of time passes without a response (shows that you consider their response to be important)
    c. keep the survey brief, the instructions simple, and the items easy to understand (if respondents become confused, they will toss the survey)
    d. make it clear that you are not trying to sell something (respondents tend to be suspicious)

7. If the response rate is very low, those who respond might be different in important ways from the target population. When this happens, it is called
    a. nonresponse bias
    b. social desirability bias
    c. confirmation bias
    d. experimenter bias

8. The Ethics Box in Chapter 12 describes the case of a female journalist who was fired after the station conducted a survey. Which of the following was true about the survey?
    a. the survey was fair but the sample was a biased sample
    b. the survey was fair and the sample appropriate, but no statistical summary was given
    c. although the results were summarized statistically, no inferential statistical analysis was completed
    d. the survey was in an interview format; a written survey would have been better

9. Which of the following was true about the Plous survey about attitudes toward the use of animals in research?
    a. professors were in favor of using animals, but students were opposed
    b. he used a stratified sampling procedure
    c. the male-female proportion of his sample matched the population proportion
    d. by asking only if respondents "supported" animal research, the survey questions were biased

10. Which of the following studies is inappropriately matched with the method used in it?
    a. comparing recovery rates for people with and without a pleasant view out the window of their hospital room – participant observation
    b. examining the extraordinary memory abilities of S. – case study
    c. comparing Burger King hamburgers with hamburgers from McDonalds – survey
    d. studying the altruistic behavior of school children – observational

11. Subject reactivity is least likely to occur in which type of study?
    a. participant observation
    b. phone survey
    c. case study
    d. archival study

12. Which of the following characterized the "room with a view" study?
    a. it was an example of structured observational research
    b. it showed that even with archival research, it is possible to randomly assign and thereby complete a true experiment
    c. it showed that independent variables can be manipulated in archival research
    d. it showed that in archival research, you have to take what you get – there is no way to control extraneous factors

Applications Exercises

12.1. Deciding on the Best Descriptive Method

To test each of the following research hypotheses, decide which of the following descriptive methods would be best to use. In some cases, it might be useful to combine more than a single method.

> Naturalistic observation (with and without structure)
> Participant observation
> Interview survey (interview, written, or phone)
> Case study
> Archival study

1. When male-female couples watch television, men control the remote more than women do. Furthermore, while this disproportion annoys women, men seem to be unaware of any problem.

2. When teenagers go to the mall, males tend to be interested in females and females tend to be interested in shopping.

3. First year college students who binge drink, compared with those who drink more moderately, are more likely to come from small towns and to have relatively little experience with alcohol when in high school.

4. After having open-heart surgery, heart patients are usually assigned to a cardiac rehabilitation program. In general, people are more faithful to the program and stay with it longer if they are (a) female rather than male, and (b) relatively more educated.

5. When 20-30 year-old male joggers run through a neighborhood, their pace will increase if there are 20-30 year-old women sitting on the porches of that neighborhood.

6. Regular attendance at church youth groups increases the level of altruism among group members.

7. Parents whose children are 9-12 years old show a high level of concern about the amount of violence on TV than parents of children aged 1-4; those parents with children aged 5-8 show an intermediate level of concern; married couples without children are generally unconcerned.

8. Following a devastating tornado in Kansas, residents are more likely to be rebuilt in the same location if they were born and raised in Kansas or another Midwestern state than if they were from the east or west coasts.

12.2. Developing Ideas for Archival Research

The following sources of information, each readily available to students, could provide data for an archival study. For each information source, create an empirical question that an archival study would hope to answer. For example,

Source: cafeteria menus
Empirical Question: Are dinner menus determined in part by what might be left over from lunch menus?

1. Source: Bulletin boards on campus
   Empirical Question:

2. Source: Graffiti on walls of rest rooms
   Empirical Question:

3. Source: Student newspaper
   Empirical Question:

4. Source: Information on professor's office doors
   Empirical Question:

5. Source: Yearbooks from high school
   Empirical Question:

Answers to Sample Test Items

<u>Fill-ins</u>

1. participant observation
2. reactivity
3. interobserver reliability
4. case study
5. closed; open-ended
6. archival
7. social desirability
8. unobtrusive measure

<u>Matching</u>

From top to bottom, the correct letter sequence is: G, I, E, H, C, D, A, F, J, B

<u>Multiple Choice</u>

1. a. this is very difficult if not impossible with most species
    b. CORRECT ANSWER – researchers assume that animals will behave naturally once they become accustomed to the observers and recognize that the observers are not a threat
    c. video recordings can be useful, in a zoo settings perhaps, but can be impractical in a field setting
    d. reactivity also occurs with animals, especially those with developed cortexes (e.g., reactivity might not be a problem with ants)

2. a. no interviews were completed
    b. CORRECT ANSWER – the observations occurred with no attempt to intervene
    c. it was naturalistic observation
    d. the observations occurred with no attempt to intervene or create a structured environment

3. a. CORRECT ANSWER – the addition of new members might have reinforced the beliefs of cult members
    b. informed consent of cult was not obtained, but that is not common practice today
    c. Festinger's observers did not have tape recorders, and memory was a problem
    d. Festinger was able to show how cults became even more committed to their message after a prophecy failed

4. a. is equally likely to occur in both types of observation
    b. can still occur with unobtrusive measures
    c. is certainly a problem, but observational research, if well done, can be used for falsification
    d. CORRECT ANSWER – especially if the checklist is precise and observers are given some training

5. a. open-ended questions and follow-up questions are actually easier with interviews
    b. question ambiguity is less of a problem because the interview can clarify vague questions on the spot
    c. CORRECT ANSWER – some bias can occur is blacks interview whites and vice versa
    d. sampling can be a problem with interviews – for example, the poor tend to be under-represented in interview surveys

6. a. CORRECT ANSWER – the opposite is true; respondents prefer surveys that can be completed quickly and simply
   b. reminders are a good idea
   c. this is also a good idea
   d. so is this

7. a. CORRECT ANSWER – the sample in this case would not be representative
   b. this occurs when respondents answer questions as they think they ought to answer them, rather than as a reflection of their true opinions or feeling
   c. not relevant - confirmation bias is a tendency to look for evidence in support of one's beliefs
   d. experimenter bias in survey research might occur if a researcher words questions in such a way as to produce a desired response

8. a. some of the surveys questions reflected bias (e.g., focusing on attractiveness instead of journalistic skills
   b. statistical analysis was done, but done inappropriately (no inferential analysis)
   c. CORRECT ANSWER – all that was reported were summary statistics
   d. the survey was in a written format

9. a. both groups were in favor; students were opposed
   b. he used a cluster sampling procedure
   c. CORRECT ANSWER – this made him feel better about the relatively low response rate
   d. Plous carefully phrased his questions to include both the words "support" and "oppose"

10. a. CORRECT ANSWER – this was an archival study
    b. this was a case study
    c. this involved a survey
    d. this was a structured observational study

11. a. observer presence could affect behavior in several ways
    b. reactivity could easily occur, especially if the surveyers asks sensitive questions
    c. likely to occur of the subject of the case study knows he or she is the object of study
    d. CORRECT ANSWER – involves information already available, so no new participants would be involved

12. a. it was an archival study
    b. groups were formed, and attempts were made to reduce the nonequivalence, but random assignment was not possible in this study
    c. CORRECT ANSWER – in the study it was possible to compare patients with a window with those not having a window
    d. the data of archival research can be limited, but some control is possible (e.g., only considering certain types of medical cases, only using patients within a certain age range

Feedback on Applications Exercises

Deciding on the Best Descriptive Method

1. This could possibly be a case study, using a small number of couples over an extended period of time. A more likely possibility is an interview survey, the interview format being better able to probe the level of female annoyance than a written or phone survey

2. Written or interview surveys could be used. It could also be done as a naturalistic observational study without structure (for instance, interest in shopping could be inferred from the number of shopping bags carried).

3. Survey research would be the simplest way to complete this study; written surveys would suffice. Survey data on drinking might be validated with reference to university disciplinary records (i.e., archival information)

4. This could be an archival study, relying on hospital records of attendance at rehab sessions; such records would also provide information about gender and level of education. There is also the possibility of doing this as a naturalistic observation study without structure or even as a participant observation study.

5. This could be done as a naturalistic observation study with structure added in the form of whether or not women were on the porch.

6. This could be a survey study (any form, but interview might yield more in-depth information on activities that could be considered altruistic. This could also be done as a participant observation study.

7. A phone survey could be adequate in this case; it could be conducted quickly and include a large sample size.

8. This could be an archival study, but might also be a case study of an event, by carefully studying the lives of a group of neighbors affected by the event; the case study could include interviews and observations.

Developing Ideas for Archival Research

There are lots of possibilities for empirical questions in these situations. Here are some possibilities:

1. Source: Bulletin boards on campus
   Empirical Question: When looking at notices of books for sale, are students more likely to sell books from core courses than from books used in courses for specific majors?

2. Source: Graffiti on walls of rest rooms
   Empirical Question: Are telephone numbers more likely to appear in graffiti in men's' rest rooms or in women's' rest rooms?

3. Source: Student newspaper
   Empirical Question: Are student newspapers at public universities more critical of university administrations than newspapers at private universities?

4. Source: Information on professor's office doors
   Empirical Question: Do the cartoons on professors' office doors indicate liberal or conservative tendencies?

Part II

LAB MANUAL

A Laboratory Manual for Doing Research in Psychology

The best way to learn how to do research in psychology is to actually do some, and this Lab Manual is designed to let you do just that. It includes a set of six data collection exercises that illustrate many of the methods found in the main text. In fact, two of the labs (4 and 5) are based on the studies described in the text. None of the exercises require special equipment or materials. The labs are as follows:

1. Creating False Memories...page 177
2. Gender Differences in Cognitive Mapping.................................. page 181
3. The Cola Wars: A Taste Test...page 187
4. Context Effects in Memory...page 189
5. Physical Attractiveness and Punishment.................................... page 192
6. Cell Phone Use and Impression Formation................................page 198

It might not be possible to complete all of these labs in your research methods course. In that event, I have also provided, for each study, a sample data set that produces an outcome that might be expected from hypothesis being tested. Your instructor might ask you to hone your data analysis skills by subjecting these data sets to the appropriate statistical analyses.

A Note on Data Collection

For each of the labs, your instructor will tell you how many participants to test, but it will probably be one participant for each condition in the experiment. To produce a sufficient amount of data for an overall analysis, your instructor will probably accumulate the data collected by each student in the class and compile them into a larger data set.

An Important Note on Research Ethics

Some of the projects in this manual can be completed by using students in the class as participants. In that case, with your instructor in charge and assigning the labs as he or she would any other class assignment, IRB approval is probably not needed. On the other hand, other labs might require a larger N and may require IRB approval in order for you to use your school's participant pool or apply some other means of recruiting volunteers who aren't members of your class.

One important guideline that you must follow is this:

THESE EXPERIMENTS MUST BE DONE UNDER THE SUPERVISION OF YOUR INSTRUCTOR.

That is, in no case should you take it upon yourself to conduct an experiment without proper supervision. To do so would be a serious violation of the APA ethics code.

As part of the supervision, your instructor will remind you about your responsibilities as an experimenter. That is, you should obtain informed consent and answer any of your participants' questions before starting, be sure to give them the opportunity to discontinue the study at any time during it, give them a thorough debriefing at the close of the session, and take clear steps to ensure their confidentiality.

Before you begin collecting any data, it would also be a good idea to review the Ethics Box in Chapter 8 of the text—"On Being a Competent and Ethical Researcher."

Laboratory 1. Creating False Memories

An important area of applied memory research concerns the extent to which memories can be wrong, even though the person feels confident about the accuracy of the memory. For example, if we show that memories can be created under certain circumstances, then questions can be raised about truth of such things as the accuracy of eyewitness memory. This first lab is designed to create a simple false memory, using a procedure similar to the one used in Robinson and Roediger (1997).

To create false memories, participants first study words that are associated with a particular concept. For instance, the words might include "bed," "rest," "snooze," and so on, but not include the associated word "sleep." When asked to recall such lists, participants often mistakenly recall sleep, and on recognition tests, they are often highly confident about having seen the word sleep on the list. Hence, a false memory of the word sleep has been created. This lab will examine the chances of producing false memories as a function of how many words on a list are related to the word sleep. Those related words will be referred to as "sleep category words"); the word SLEEP, not on the list but associated with the sleep category words, is called a "critical lure."

The between-subjects independent variable in this study will be the number of list words that are associated with the critical lure (SLEEP) and there will be four levels. Each list will have 15 words on it, with either 0, 5, 10, or 15 sleep category words. The lists will be structured like this:

List 1: 0 sleep category words and 15 words unrelated to the critical lure
List 2: 5 sleep category words and 10 words unrelated to the critical lure
List 3: 10 sleep category words and 5 words unrelated to the critical lure
List 4: 15 sleep category words and 0 words unrelated to the critical lure

Procedure

Your instructor will tell you how many participants to recruit, but it will probably be at least four for each student in the lab (one participant for each condition). Randomly assign the four volunteers to one of the four conditions and follow the normal informed consent procedures in place at your school. After each list has been studied, give participants a 2-minute distractor task (e.g., a sheet of paper with simple addition problems should do the trick). To test for false memories, give them the recognition test on page 179 (make as many copies as you need). The test is appropriate for all four lists, so it can be given to participants in all four groups. Be sure that in addition to circling the items they thought they studied, they should also rate how confident they were about having seen every one of the items in the recognition test. These ratings will range from 1 to 5. For uncircled words, the rating provides an indication of how certain participants are that the word was NOT on the list. For circled words, the rating indicates how certain participants are that the word WAS on the list. For instance, if they don't circle a word and give it a "5," it means that they are very confident that the word was not on the list; if they circle a word and give it a "2," it means they thought the word was on the list, but they aren't very confident about their judgment.

So that you can see how the lists are organized, I have underlined the sleep category words in each list on the next page. When you present the lists to participants, however, do not highlight these key words in any way. You can present the lists in one of two ways. First (preferred), you can present the words visually. This could be done by printing each word on a single 3x5 file card, them turning the cards over one at a time at a constant rate (2 sec/item is good—saying "1001, 1002, turn" to yourself is adequate). You could also present them all at once, on a single sheet of paper, and give participants a fixed amount of time (28 seconds is good—you'll need a stopwatch or a watch with a second hand for this procedure) to study the words. If you have experience with PowerPoint, you could also present the materials in a timed presentation, with one word per slide. A second presentation strategy is to read the words to participants, again at a constant rate (this is harder than flipping cars at a constant rate though). Regardless of the method you choose, practice on a friend first. The task for your participants is to study the words and to be prepared to recall as many as they can, in any order (in fact, however, they will be doing a recognition test instead of a recall test). That is, you should instruct your participants to memorize the list while it is being presented. Here are the lists. The sleep category words were taken from a false memory demonstration described in Payne and Wenger (1998).

The important outcome, of course, is how many times the word "SLEEP" is circled on the recognition test, even though it was presented. The number of participants falsely recognizing it should increase from List 1 through List 4. Average confidence ratings for SLEEP should also increase from List 1 through List 4. The study uses a single-factor, multi-level, independent groups design (Chapter 7).

Here are the lists:

	0/15 *List 1*	5/10 *List 2*	10/5 *List 3*	0/15 *List 4*
1	mad	bed	bed	bed
2	white	white	rest	rest
3	butter	butter	butter	awake
4	table	tired	tired	tired
5	low	low	hot	dream
6	nurse	nurse	wake	wake
7	shoe	snooze	snooze	snooze
8	apple	apple	apple	blanket
9	boy	boy	doze	doze
10	hot	hot	slumber	slumber
11	queen	snore	snore	snore
12	hill	hill	hill	nap
13	thread	thread	peace	peace
14	water	yawn	yawn	yawn
15	door	door	door	drowsy

Analysis

The primary outcome of interest is the recognition frequency, in each of the four conditions, for the critical lure sleep. Frequency data means a nominal scale of measurement (Chapter 4 in the text) and the proper analysis is a Chi-square test for goodness of fit. See Appendix C in the text for instructions about how to complete this analysis.

A secondary analysis concerns the confidence ratings for the recognition of the word SLEEP. First, take all the cases in which SLEEP was not circled and change the scores all to minus scores (e.g., a "3" becomes a "-3"). Then, for the critical lure SLEEP, calculate a mean confidence score for the participants in each of the four groups and compare the means with a 1-way ANOVA for independent groups (Appendix C). If the ANOVA is significant, follow the analysis with a post hoc analysis (Tukey's HSD is the example used in Appendix C).

Recognition Test

The following list of words includes some that were on the list you just studied and others that were not on the list. First, circle each of the words that you think was on the list. Then, in front of every word on the test, write a number from 1 to 5. For those words that you have circled, the number indicates how confident you are that the word WAS on the list you studied (the higher the number, the greater the confidence that you studied the word). For those words that you have NOT circled, the number indicates how confident you are that the word WAS NOT on the list you studied (the higher the number, the greater the confidence that you did not study the word).

blanket	hot	bed	mad
butter	slumber	sick	rest
dream	white	husband	boy
valley	peace	sleep	wake
shoe	snooze	table	apple
legs	pin	hill	door
fear	low	doze	drowsy
tired	water	orange	nurse
awake	snore	queen	robber
thread	yawn	toe	nap

SAMPLE DATA SET – Creating False Memories

In the event that you do not have the opportunity to complete the false memory study, here are some hypothetical data that the study might have produced. Perform the statistical analysis described in the instructions for the lab and draw a conclusion about the study's outcome.

Assume an N of 20 in each group.

The number of participants in each group falsely recognizing the critical lure (SLEEP) was:

Group 1 (0/15):   3
Group 2 (5/10):   3
Group 3 (10/5):   11
Group 4 (15/0):   16

Confidence ratings (minus numbers indicate instances when the critical lure was not chosen):

Part. #	Group 1 (0/15)	Group 2 (5/10)	Group 3 (10/5)	Group 4 (15/0)
1	-5	+4	+3	+3
2	-5	-2	+2	+4
3	-4	-4	-1	+2
4	-3	-5	+5	-4
5	-5	-1	+3	+1
6	-1	-1	-5	+2
7	-2	+3	-4	+3
8	-3	-2	-1	-3
9	-3	-4	+4	+5
10	-3	+3	-1	+4
11	+3	-5	-2	+2
12	-5	-1	+3	-5
13	-4	-1	+5	+1
14	-1	-1	-2	+1
15	-1	-3	-3	+4
16	-2	-2	+4	+3
17	-3	-3	+3	-1
18	+2	-5	-2	+3
19	-5	-5	+1	+2
20	+2	-2	+5	+2

Laboratory 2. Gender Differences in Cognitive Mapping

As we become familiar with a geographic environment, we develop what experimental psychologists call a cognitive map. Consider a college or university campus, for example. A cognitive map of a campus contains information about how far it is from one building to another, where each building stands in relation to others, the locations of prominent landmarks, and how to get from one place to another by the shortest route. Researchers studying cognitive maps have often found gender differences in how these maps are organized and in the strategies used to navigate through environments. For example, males often use what has been called an "orientation" strategy (Lawton, 1996). This means that they rely on general cardinal directions (north, etc.) when finding their way from one place to another. It also means they tend to feel confident about their overall "sense of direction" and, if they get lost, they seem to know (or think they know) the general direction they should be heading. Females, on the other hand, often use what Lawton (1996) called a "route" strategy, in which they move through the environment by relying on landmarks and other specific information about a route to be followed (e.g., go three blocks and turn left at the bookstore). In this lab, you will compare males and females on their (a) self assessed sense of direction, (b) degree of anxiety about spatial skills, and (c) preferred strategy—orientation or route—for navigating through the environment. Because gender is a subject variable (see Chapter 5 in the text), the design is a nonequivalent groups design (Chapter 7).

Procedure

Your instructor will tell you how many males and females to recruit for the study. Give each participant the following tasks (make as many copies as you need). Present the tests in a random order to each person who participates.

1.   Sense of Direction Estimate (1-10)

2.   Spatial Anxiety Scale

3.   Wayfinding Strategy Scale

Score the two Lawton scales as follows:

Spatial Anxiety Scale. Simply add up the numbers circled by participants. Scores will range from 8-40.

Wayfinding Strategy Scale. This survey yields two scores, one for an orientation strategy and one for a route strategy. For the Orientation Strategy score, add up the numbers circled for items #3, 4, 5, 9, 10, 11, 12, 13, & 14. For the Route Strategy score, add up the numbers circled for items #1, 2, 6, 7, & 8.

Analysis

For each of the four dependent variables—sense of direction, spatial anxiety, orientation strategy, and route strategy—compare males and females by completing a t test for independent groups. Then create a correlation matrix by correlating (Pearson's r) each variable with every other variable.

Note: The Spatial Anxiety Scale and the Wayfinding Strategy Scale are being used with the kind permission of Dr. Carol Lawton, Psychology Department, Indiana University Purdue University Fort Wayne. To complete this laboratory exercise, you have her permission to make as many copies as you need. If you wish to use either scale in a project outside of the research methods course you are now taking, however, you will have to seek her permission to do so.

Sense of Direction

When people say they have a good sense of direction, they generally mean that they don't often get lost, that they have a good idea about how to get from one location to another, and that they can find their way around a geographical environment once they have been exposed to that environment once or twice. With that as a general idea about sense of direction, how would you rate yours?

1	2	3	4	5	6	7	8	9	10

very
poor

very
good

Spatial Anxiety Scale

Rate the level of anxiety you think you would feel in each of the situations below. Use the following scale to rate your level of anxiety. That is, circle a number corresponding to the level of anxiety you think you would feel in each of the listed situations.

LEVEL OF ANXIETY:
    1 = not at all
    2 = a little
    3 = a fair amount
    4 = much
    5 = very much

1 2 3 4 5   1. Finding your way to an appointment in an area of a city or town with which you are not familiar.

1 2 3 4 5   2. Finding your way out of a complex arrangement of offices that you have visited for the first time.

1 2 3 4 5   3. Finding your way around an unfamiliar mall.

1 2 3 4 5   4. Finding your way back to a familiar area after realizing you have made a wrong turn and become lost while driving.

1 2 3 4 5   5. Pointing in the direction of a place outside that someone wants to get to and has asked you for directions, when you are in a windowless room.

1 2 3 4 5   6. Locating your car in a very large parking lot or parking garage.

1 2 3 4 5   7. Leaving a store that you have been to for the first time and deciding which way to turn to get to a destination.

1 2 3 4 5   8. Trying a new route that you think will be a shortcut without the benefit of a map.

Wayfinding Strategy Scale

Think of times in the past when you have driven for the first time to a specific location in a SOMEWHAT FAMILIAR city or town (i.e., you had been to the city a few times before, but never to that particular location within the city). Rate each of the following strategies for how likely you were to use it in this type of situation. If the strategy is not at all typical of you, circle the "1"; if the strategy is extremely typical of you, circle the "5" oval, etc.

1	2	3	4	5
not at all typical of me		moderately typical of me		extremely typical of me

1. I made a mental note of landmarks, such as buildings or natural features, that I passed along the way.
   1   2   3   4   5

2. Before starting, I asked for directions telling me how many streets to pass before making each turn.
   1   2   3   4   5

3. I visualized a map or layout of the area in my mind as I drove.
   1   2   3   4   5

4. I referred to a published road map.
   1   2   3   4   5

5. I kept track of the direction (north, south, east, or west) in which I was going.
   1   2   3   4   5

6. Before starting, I asked for a hand-drawn map of the area.
   1   2   3   4   5

7. As I drove, I made a mental note of the number of streets I passed before making each turn.
   1   2   3   4   5

8. Before starting, I asked for directions telling me whether to turn right or left at particular streets or landmarks.
   1   2   3   4   5

9. I kept track of where I was in relation to the sun (or moon) in the sky as I went.
   1   2   3   4   5

10. As I drove, I made a mental note of the mileage I traveled on different roads.
    1   2   3   4   5

11. I kept track of the relationship between where I was and the center of town.
    1   2   3   4   5

12. Before starting, I asked for directions telling me whether to go east, west, north, or south at particular streets or landmarks.
    1   2   3   4   5

13. Before starting, I asked for directions telling me how far to go in terms of mileage.
    1   2   3   4   5

14. Kept track of the relationship between where I was and the next place where I had to change direction.
    1   2   3   4   5

SAMPLE DATA SET – Gender Differences in Cognitive Mapping

In the event that you do not have the opportunity to complete the cognitive mapping lab, here are some hypothetical data that the study might have produced. Perform the statistical analysis described in the instructions and draw a conclusion about the study's outcome.

Assume an N of 40, 20 males and 20 females.

Data for the Males:

Part. #	Sense of Direction	Spatial Anxiety	Orientation Strategy	Route Strategy
1	9	20	37	6
2	4	16	36	18
3	8	19	25	7
4	7	23	37	24
5	6	14	21	15
6	8	15	29	13
7	9	23	27	9
8	7	10	36	12
9	8	17	35	10
10	7	15	26	18
11	6	13	32	12
12	8	18	24	17
13	8	14	37	16
14	8	26	38	18
15	7	15	28	15
16	6	12	34	21
17	9	14	26	7
18	8	19	43	17
19	5	21	38	12
20	8	17	32	14

Data for the Males:

Part. #	Sense of Direction	Spatial Anxiety	Orientation Strategy	Route Strategy
1	6	30	29	19
2	5	21	21	23
3	6	29	23	24
4	8	24	27	25
5	5	33	24	20
6	2	24	19	24
7	4	23	30	21
8	5	26	29	16
9	6	19	23	21
10	7	20	26	15
11	5	38	22	13
12	7	22	21	24
13	6	25	24	23
14	8	24	17	19
15	7	23	24	20
16	6	28	19	25
17	5	26	26	18
18	7	20	23	16
19	5	18	32	18
20	6	26	24	20

Laboratory 3. The Cola Wars: A Taste Test

Competing producers of cola products always seem to claim that their drink is the best and will be preferred by others in "taste tests." Such tests are often biased in ways favoring the cola company sponsoring the taste test, however. Lab 4 uses a double blind procedure and the proper use of counterbalancing to yield an unbiased assessment of the relative merits of two cola products (Coke and Pepsi will be the examples used in the narrative, but any two varieties will do).

In order for the double blind procedure to be effective, the study will require two experimenters, one to set up the tasting sequences and a second to actually test the participants. The experimenter setting up the procedure will pour equal amounts of the drinks into same-sized paper cups and place the cups on a table at which a participant will sit. Each participant will test four drinks and the drinks will be presented in a sequence determined by a reverse counterbalancing procedure.

Half of the participants will receive this sequence:

Coke – Pepsi – Pepsi – Coke   [CPPC]

The remaining participants will receive this sequence:

Pepsi – Coke – Coke – Pepsi   [PCCP]

Procedure

You will need a supply of Coke, Pepsi, paper cups, and unflavored crackers. The first experimenter (E1) will prepare the drinks in precisely measured and equal amounts in unmarked paper cups, and lines them up in the proper sequence. The second experimenter (E2) will run the participants through the procedure. So that E2 won't know which cola is in which cup, E1 must determine ahead of time whether participants will be given the CPPC sequence or the PCCP sequence. If there are to be twenty participants tested (your instructor will tell you how many people to test), half should get CPPC and half should get PCCP. The sequences can be alternated, but only if the sequence presented to the first participant is determined randomly (a coin toss will do) and is not known by E2.

E2 will test the participants, who should be told that they will be trying four different cola drinks (slight deception here—they are only rating two different drinks, of course) and rating the drinks in several ways. Each participant should drink all of the liquid from the first cup, then give a response for each of the three rating scales. After completing the first drink, the participant will eat a cracker to remove any lingering aftertaste of the first drink, and then sample the second drink. This sequence of drink—rate—cracker will continue until all four of the drinks have been sampled.

After tasting each drink, participants give verbal ratings for sweetness, aftertaste, and overall liking. That is, after drink has been consumed, E2 will ask (and record the verbal responses):

1. On a scale from 1-10, with 1 meaning not at all sweet and 10 meaning extremely sweet, how would you rate the sweetness of the cola you just drank?

2. On a scale from 1-10, with 1 meaning no aftertaste and 10 meaning a very strong aftertaste, how would you rate the aftertaste strength of the cola you just drank?

3. On a scale from 1-10, with 1 meaning strong dislike and 10 meaning a strong liking, how would you rate the overall quality of the cola you just drank?

Analysis

For each participant, combine the ratings for each of the two drinks that were the same brand. The combined data will yield, for each participant, a 20-point scale for sweetness, aftertaste, and quality for both drinks. These data can be analyzed with three (one for each scale) different t tests for dependent groups.

SAMPLE DATA SET – The Cola Wars: A Taste Test

In the event that you do not have the opportunity to complete the taste test, here are some hypothetical data that the study might have produced. Perform the statistical analysis described in the instructions and draw a conclusion about the study's outcome.

Assume an N of 20. Each score is a combined rating for two samples of the same product, with a range from 1 to 20.

Part. #	Sweetness ratings		Aftertaste ratings		Overall Liking	
	Coke	Pepsi	Coke	Pepsi	Coke	Pepsi
1	12	14	9	4	15	13
2	10	16	15	3	16	15
3	11	12	14	9	14	14
4	9	18	12	8	13	16
5	14	15	9	7	10	12
6	13	13	8	7	18	18
7	7	17	16	6	13	15
8	6	16	12	9	16	17
9	10	12	14	10	17	11
10	12	11	13	9	12	17
11	15	16	8	6	16	12
12	7	18	10	8	11	18
13	8	17	11	3	10	16
14	8	14	15	7	12	12
15	6	15	13	9	10	10
16	11	14	9	6	13	12
17	15	16	7	8	9	16
18	12	13	12	5	14	13
19	10	11	10	13	16	18
20	8	12	11	5	17	15

Laboratory 4. Context Effects in Memory

Chapter 8 includes a study by Godden and Baddeley (1975) that illustrates the importance of context on our ability to learn and recall verbal information. Divers showed much better recall if their recall environment (on a beach or underwater) matched their study environment than if there was a mismatch (e.g., they did poorly if they studied on land and recalled under the water). Laboratory 3 will use essentially the same design but examine a different kind of context—whether or not music is present during study and recall phases of the study. That is, there will be four different conditions in this 2x2 independent groups design:

Condition 1. Study with Music – Recall with Music

Condition 2. Study with Music – Recall without Music

Condition 3. Study without Music – Recall with Music

Condition 4. Study without Music – Recall without Music

In addition to examining the general influence of context, notice that the study also looks at the issue of whether the presence of music can influence our ability to study and recall verbal information. A comparison of conditions 1 and 4 looks at the overall influence of music on memory.

The choice of music is up to you, but it might be best to avoid dissonant sounds that would distract the participant. Familiar selections from classical music would be a good choice, and if you pick something from Mozart, your results might even bear on the alleged Mozart effect that is examined critically in Chapter 7 (Case Study #11).

Procedure

Your instructor will tell you how many participants to recruit, but it will probably be at least four (one participant for each condition). Randomly assign the four volunteers to one of the four conditions and follow the normal informed consent procedures in place at your school. Participants should be told that the study has to do with the effects of music on memory—otherwise they will be confused when you turn on the music in the first three conditions. Those in the fourth condition should also be told the general purpose, but they can be informed that they are in a control group (no music).

Make copies of the 30-item word list on the next page. The words are 1- and 2-syllable high frequency unrelated (relatively) concrete nouns. Give the list to participants to study, but hand it to them with the page turned over so they cannot see the words until you give a signal. Tell them they will have two minutes to study the list, about 4 seconds per word. They can study them using any method they would like, and they should be informed that when it is time to recall the words, they will be able to recall them in any order that occurs to them. When participants are ready, tell them to turn over the word list page and begin studying. At that same moment, turn on the music for conditions 1 and 2. After two minutes, tell them to stop studying and, in conditions 1 and 2, turn off the music. To clear out lingering information in working memory, give participants a 2-minute distractor task (e.g., a sheet of paper with simple addition problems should do the trick) before starting the recall task. Then give them a clean sheet of paper and tell them to write down as many of the words as they can recall, in any order. In conditions 1 and 3, turn on the music during the recall phase. Let them recall for two minutes (it will be more than enough time). In condition 1, rewind the tape while students are completing the distractor task. This insures that the music played during recall is the same music played during the study interval.

Analysis

Simply add up the total number of words recalled for each participant, making sure that you only count words that were actually presented (sometimes people recall words that sounded like or had meanings similar to the words on the list). Analysis the data with a 2x2 independent groups ANOVA.

JACKET	SNOW	RECORD
CORN	PACKAGE	SEASON
LEG	TOOL	ENGINE
SALT	ISLAND	MONEY
JUNGLE	BABY	TEMPLE
TOWN	GATE	GUEST
PLANET	SHED	COW
ROCK	MACHINE	LOBBY
NEST	POET	NOSE
FORK	CANDY	NEST

SAMPLE DATA SET – Context Effects in Memory

In the event that you do not have the opportunity to complete the experiment on context and memory, here are some hypothetical data that the study might have produced. Perform the statistical analysis described in the instructions and draw a conclusion about the study's outcome.

Assume an N of 20 per group. Each score represents the number of words recalled out of a maximum of 30.

Group 1 = Study with Music – Recall with Music

Group 2 = Study with Music – Recall without Music

Group 3 = Study without Music – Recall with Music

Group 4 = Study without Music – Recall without Music

Part. #	Group 1	Group 2	Group 3	Group 4
1	30	12	18	23
2	13	10	19	26
3	24	8	12	25
4	26	15	14	15
5	25	18	20	19
6	22	17	16	17
7	19	16	13	16
8	17	13	7	18
9	23	15	11	25
10	18	17	15	24
11	21	9	10	16
12	27	19	23	18
13	24	14	18	20
14	17	7	12	13
15	20	18	19	21
16	20	19	14	26
17	26	12	16	17
18	24	16	13	19
19	18	14	19	19
20	22	13	11	23

Laboratory 5. Physical Attractiveness and Punishment

Chapter 6 in the textbook briefly describes a study by Sigall and Ostrove (1975), in which participants read descriptions of two crimes and recommended punishment for "Barbara Helm," the woman committing the crimes. The study is an early and well-known example of research that examines how variables that should not influence judicial decisions might nonetheless have an effect. In the Barbara Helm case, one variable of interest was the degree of her physical attractiveness. A second variable was the type of crime committed, a burglary or a swindle, each involving $2,200. The design was a 2x3 independent groups factorial—two crime types and three levels of attractiveness. The latter variable was manipulated by attaching a photo to the crime description that participants read. One group saw a photo of a very attractive Barbara Helm, a second group saw an unattractive Barbara, and a third (control) group did not see a photo at all. Sigall and Ostrove (1975) found an interesting interaction between crime type and attractiveness. When the crime was a theft, being attractive helped Barbara—the simulated judges (i.e., the participants) gave her a lighter sentence than when she was attractive. When the crime was a swindle, however, an attractive Barbara received a stiffer sentence. Participants apparently believed that she used her attractiveness to commit the crime.

The purpose of this lab is to replicate the findings of the Sigall and Ostrove (1975) study, with one important change. Instead of judging "Barbara Helm," your participants will judge "Justin Helm." That is, the purpose will be to determine if the Sigall and Ostrove result would occur with a male defendant and a female victim. The study will also be a 2x3 independent groups factorial. Because this means six different groups and a considerable amount of data collecting, your instructor might decide to use just one type of crime and simply compare levels of attractiveness for that particular crime. The following instructions assume that the full 2x3 study will be completed, however.

Procedure

The crime descriptions are the same ones used by Sigall and Ostrove (1975), slightly updated (e.g., $22,000 instead of $2,200). The photos are from a larger set that I pilot tested for perceived levels of attractiveness. Of twelve photos shown to a group of female undergraduates (N=25), the two selected for this lab were rated the most and the least attractive. All twelve of the photos were taken from the FBI website containing fugitives from justice.

Your instructor will probably ask you to test six different people, one per condition. You might be asked to test twelve, however—one male and one female per condition. This procedure will insure an equal number of males and females per group. Although Sigall and Ostrove (1975) found no difference in outcome between male and female participants in their study, it is a good idea to control for possible gender differences in a study like this one. Randomly assign participants to each of the conditions and ask them to read the description of the crime and answer the question at the bottom of the page. Make as many copies of the materials as you need. Copy the page with the photos, cut them out, and attach them to the appropriate descriptions with a paper clip.

Analysis

The dependent measure is the number of years recommended as a sentence for the crime. The analysis will be a 2x3 independent groups ANOVA, followed by post hoc testing if necessary.

Note: The crime descriptions are reprinted here in slightly modified form with the kind permission of Dr. Harold Sigall, Psychology Department, University of Maryland. To complete this laboratory exercise, you have his permission to make as many copies as you need. If you wish to use the descriptions in a project outside of the research methods course you are now taking, however, you will have to seek his permission to do so.

CASE 98-103586

Name: Justin Robert Helm

Age: 31

Height: 6'1"   Weight: 190

Place of Birth: Chicago, Illinois

Marital Status: Single

On July 7, 1998, Justin Helm was arrested and subsequently indicted on criminal charges of obtaining money under false pretenses and grand larceny. Mr. Helm was charged with illegally obtaining $22,000 (twenty-two thousand dollars) from Ms. Charlotte Tyler, for the presumed purpose of investing that sum in Southwestern Software, Incorporated, a non-existent corporation. Both Mr. Helm and Ms. Tyler resided in the Regency Towers, a high-rise apartment building in St. Louis, Missouri.

Ms. Tyler had lived at the Regency Towers for three years at the time the crime was committed. Mr. Helm, on the other hand, had moved into his apartment when he first arrived in town, approximately two months before the date of the crime. Neighbors who were questioned by authorities said that their contact with him was slight, but that he seemed pleasant and had not caused any trouble. According to one neighbor, Mr. Helm claimed to be looking for full time employment.

Mr. Helm apparently singled out Charlotte Tyler, 46, an unmarried office manager, as a likely prospect and watched her movements for some time. He contrived to meet her several times on the elevator, once invited her to his apartment for coffee, and after having solidified these initial contacts, asked her for some advice concerning an investment he claimed to have made in Southwestern Software, Inc. He showed her related literature and stressed the attractiveness of the stock. When she indicated moderate interest he informed her of his willingness to invest any amount, however small, for her. Subsequently Ms. Tyler wrote a check for $22,000 made out to the corporation for 1,000 shares of stock. That same evening Mr. Helm informed Ms. Tyler that he would be leaving in a few days for a two-week vacation, and that although he would see to it that her money was invested, it would be a week to 10 days until she received the stock certificates in the mail. When the stock certificates failed to arrive, Ms. Tyler waited until Mr. Helm's expected date of return to tell him that she had not received the certificates. She could not find him, and upon checking with the building's management, she learned that he had suddenly moved out, two weeks earlier, leaving no forwarding address. She immediately called the police.

After an extensive investigation, Mr. Helm was located and apprehended in Chicago, Illinois. Extradition was waived and he was returned St. Louis for indictment and to stand trail. In a jury trial, Justin Helm was found guilty as charged.

Complete the following statement by circling a number between 1 and 15, corresponding to the number of years you believe the defendant, Justin Helm, should serve in prison. Assume he has been convicted of the crime you just read about.

I would sentence the defendant, Justin Helm, to ____ years of imprisonment.

1   2   3   4   5   6   7   8   9   10   11   12   13   14   15

CASE 98-103586

Name: Justin Robert Helm

Age: 31

Height: 6'1"   Weight: 190

Place of Birth: Chicago, Illinois

Marital Status: Single

On July 7, 1998, Justin Helm was arrested and subsequently indicted on criminal charges of breaking and entering, and grand larceny. Mr. Helm was charged with illegally entering the apartment of Ms. Charlotte Tyler and stealing a gold watch, two rings, other assorted pieces of jewelry, a large valuable coin collection, and $525 in cash, from her. The total loss was estimated to be $22,000 (twenty-two thousand dollars). Both Mr. Helm and Ms. Tyler resided in the Regency Towers, a high-rise apartment building in St. Louis, Missouri.

Ms. Tyler had lived at the Regency Towers for three years at the time the crime was committed. Mr. Helm, on the other hand, had moved into his apartment when he first arrived in town, approximately two months before the date of the crime. Neighbors who were questioned by authorities said that their contact with him was slight, but that he seemed pleasant and had not caused any trouble. According to one neighbor, Mr. Helm claimed to be looking for full-time employment.

Mr. Helm seems to have singled out Charlotte Tyler, 46, an unmarried office manager, as a likely prospect and watched her movements for some time. On the night of June 16, after she had left her home for her weekly session at a local gymnasium, Mr. Helm apparently entered her apartment and committed the theft. Ms. Tyler discovered the loss when she returned home, and immediately contacted the police.

Mr. Helm was apprehended in Chicago about three weeks later. Hardly anyone other than the building's management had noticed that he had moved from the Regency Towers four days after the crime. The police had circulated descriptions of the stolen articles, and when Mr. Helm attempted to sell the coin collection, the dealer recognized the collection and called the police. The coin dealer stalled for time until the police arrived and arrested Helm. A warrant was obtained and Mr. Helm's apartment was searched. In addition to the pieces of jewelry, a passkey to all apartments in the Regency Tower was discovered. Mr. Helm waived extradition and was returned to St. Louis to stand trial. During the investigation the building's manager revealed that about ten days prior to the date of the crime Mr. Helm had come to him, told him he had misplaced the key to his apartment and asked to borrow the pass key— he returned the pass key two or three hours later that same day. The manager had not attached any special significance to this episode because residents frequently borrowed the pass key in similar situations. In a jury trial, Justin Helm was found guilty as charged.

Complete the following statement by circling a number between 1 and 15, corresponding to the number of years you believe the defendant, Justin Helm, should serve in prison. Assume he has been convicted of the crime you just read about.

I would sentence the defendant, Justin Helm, to ___ years of imprisonment.

1   2   3   4   5   6   7   8   9   10   11   12   13   14   15

Photos to be used in the Justin Helm cases:

Attractive Justin Helm:

Unattractive Justin Helm:

SAMPLE DATA SET – Physical Attractiveness and the Assignment of Punishment

In the event that you do not have the opportunity to complete the Justin Helm—Charlotte Tyler experiment, here are some hypothetical data that the study might have produced. Perform the statistical analysis described in the instructions and draw a conclusion about the study's outcome.

Assume an N=20 per group. Each score equals the number of years sentenced, out of a maximum of 15.

      Group 1 = Swindle – Attractive Justin Helm (Sw-A)

      Group 2 = Swindle – Unattractive Justin Helm (Sw-U)

      Group 3 = Swindle – No photo of Justin Helm (Sw-N)

      Group 4 = Burglary – Attractive Justin Helm (Bu-A)

      Group 5 = Burglary – Unattractive Justin Helm (Bu-U)

      Group 6 = Burglary – No photo of Justin Helm (Bu-N)

Part.#	Sw-U	Sw-U	Sw-N	Bu-A	Bu-U	Bu-N
1	8	6	8	6	7	6
2	6	4	6	4	8	8
3	7	8	5	3	9	6
4	8	6	6	6	7	7
5	4	9	4	7	6	6
6	6	4	8	5	6	9
7	8	7	6	4	6	8
8	11	5	7	5	5	5
9	7	4	6	6	3	6
10	3	7	7	4	4	7
11	6	6	4	3	5	5
12	9	3	3	6	8	8
13	6	10	6	5	8	4
14	10	6	7	4	4	7
15	8	9	10	3	5	8
16	9	7	6	4	7	7
17	10	8	4	5	10	5
18	7	6	8	4	9	9
19	8	4	6	5	10	8
20	8	7	9	6	7	4

Laboratory 6. Cell Phone Use and Impression Formation

Social psychologists have known for some time that impression formation, our tendency to make judgments about someone's personality, ability, and character can be strongly influenced by our initial contacts with people. That is, first impressions count. This final lab will examine how our impressions can be affected by current technology—the ever-present cellular telephone. Cell phones have become a part of everyday life for millions of Americans. They are both a great convenience for the person who needs assistance on the highway and a great annoyance for the person hoping to have quiet meal in a restaurant. The empirical question to be answered in Lab 6 is whether the presence of a cell phone will influence our initial impressions of a person, in this case a college-aged male. Participants will examine one of three photos of a person trying to contact another student, either by cell phone, regular phone, or via email.

Procedure

Pages 198-200 show the stimulus materials to be used in the study. Make as many copies as you need. Photo 1 shows a college-aged male in casual dress using a cell phone. As you can see from the description at the top of the page, participants are told that he is trying to call another student about a homework assignment. Photo 2 shows the same person making the same call, but from a non-cellular phone. Photo 3 shows the same person sending an email to another student. Hence, the design is one factor, multilevel design with independent groups. Little research exists on how people perceive those using cell phones, but one preliminary study has suggested that such people are perceived as having a need for control and a sense of self-importance (O'Connell and Blass, 2000).

Your instructor will probably ask you to recruit three participants and randomly assign them to one of the three conditions in the study. Follow normal consent procedures, and then give each participant a copy of one of the stimulus pages. Each page has the appropriate photo. After examining the picture, participants give their initial impressions of the person in the picture by responding to a series of bipolar scales.

Analysis

Subject the data in each of the bipolar scales to a 1-way independent groups ANOVA, followed by post hoc analysis (e.g., Tukey's HSD test) if necessary. Notice on the data sheets that a large score does not necessarily mean a greater amount of the quality in question. For instance, a high score on the first attribute indicates very little confidence, whereas a high score on attribute two suggests a great deal of intelligence. The reason for this arrangement is to avoid a type of "response bias" in which participants perceive one side a scale as "good" and the other as "bad." This perception might lead them to simply move quickly down the list, circling numbers at one end of the scale, instead of carefully considering each attribute. The important thing to be careful about is the manner in which you report your results. For instance, be careful not to report a high score on the first attribute as an indication of a great deal of confidence.

Impression Formation

Whenever we see someone for the first time, we often make an initial, if tentative, impression of that individual's personality. Imagine that you have just entered a room and observed the student pictured here. Assume that he is calling another student to ask to ask about a homework assignment. What would your initial impression be of the person? Respond by circling a number from 1 to 7 on each of the bipolar scales below the picture.

Confident	1	2	3	4	5	6	7	**Lacks confidence**
Not intelligent	1	2	3	4	5	6	7	**Intelligent**
Extraverted	1	2	3	4	5	6	7	**Introverted**
Low need to control	1	2	3	4	5	6	7	**High need to control**
Anxious	1	2	3	4	5	6	7	**Calm**
Low self-importance	1	2	3	4	5	6	7	**High self-importance**
Prefers to be with others	1	2	3	4	5	6	7	**Prefers to be alone**

Impression Formation

Whenever we see someone for the first time, we often make an initial, if tentative, impression of that individual's personality. Imagine that you have just entered a room and observed the student pictured here. Assume that he is calling another student to ask to ask about a homework assignment. What would your initial impression be of the person? Respond by circling a number from 1 to 7 on each of the bipolar scales below the picture.

Confident	1	2	3	4	5	6	7	Lacks confidence
Not intelligent	1	2	3	4	5	6	7	Intelligent
Extraverted	1	2	3	4	5	6	7	Introverted
Low need to control	1	2	3	4	5	6	7	High need to control
Anxious	1	2	3	4	5	6	7	Calm
Low self-importance	1	2	3	4	5	6	7	High self-importance
Prefers to be with others	1	2	3	4	5	6	7	Prefers to be alone

Impression Formation

Whenever we see someone for the first time, we often make an initial, if tentative, impression of that individual's personality. Imagine that you have just entered a room and observed the student pictured here. Assume that he is emailing another student to ask to ask about a homework assignment. What would your initial impression be of the person? Respond by circling a number from 1 to 7 on each of the bipolar scales below the picture.

Confident	1	2	3	4	5	6	7	Lacks confidence
Not intelligent	1	2	3	4	5	6	7	Intelligent
Extraverted	1	2	3	4	5	6	7	Introverted
Low need to control	1	2	3	4	5	6	7	High need to control
Anxious	1	2	3	4	5	6	7	Calm
Low self-importance	1	2	3	4	5	6	7	High self-importance
Prefers to be with others	1	2	3	4	5	6	7	Prefers to be alone

SAMPLE DATA SET – Cell Phone Use and Impression Formation

In the event that you do not have the opportunity to complete the cell phone experiment, here are some hypothetical data that the study might have produced. Perform the statistical analysis described in the instructions and draw a conclusion about the study's outcome.

Assume an N=20 per group. Each score equals the number of years sentenced, out of a maximum of 15.

Group CP = student using cell phone
Group RP = student using regular phone
Group EM = student using email

Scales:
conf. = degree of confidence
Intell. = intelligence level
Intro = introverted/extraverted tendencies
Cont. = level of need for control
Anx. = level of anxiety
Imp. = degree of self-importance
Greg. = degree of gregariousness

Group CP

Part.#	conf.	intell.	intro.	cont.	anx.	imp.	greg.
1	7	7	3	6	4	6	2
2	4	7	4	5	3	6	3
3	5	6	1	7	6	7	4
4	7	7	2	5	5	5	1
5	5	6	1	6	4	7	2
6	4	5	2	6	1	7	5
7	7	7	1	7	2	5	2
8	4	6	1	5	5	5	3
9	4	7	4	6	4	6	2
10	7	4	5	6	3	5	4
11	5	5	3	5	2	6	1
12	6	5	2	4	5	6	2
13	4	7	3	5	6	6	2
14	7	5	5	6	5	6	3
15	6	6	2	5	4	6	2
16	3	6	3	5	7	3	1
17	6	7	2	7	4	6	4
18	6	7	5	6	5	5	1
19	4	6	4	6	6	4	2
20	7	6	3	6	5	7	3

Group RP

Part.#	conf.	intell.	intro.	cont.	anx.	imp.	greg.
1	3	5	6	1	5	5	5
2	6	6	5	2	3	6	4
3	2	6	2	1	4	3	2
4	4	5	3	2	1	2	3
5	6	6	1	1	2	5	6
6	2	7	4	1	5	6	5
7	3	7	3	2	6	4	4
8	5	7	1	2	7	2	3
9	3	6	4	3	4	6	5
10	2	6	2	2	1	3	4
11	4	7	4	1	2	2	5
12	3	7	3	2	6	5	2
13	5	6	1	4	3	2	5
14	6	6	4	3	2	4	6
15	4	6	2	2	5	3	4
16	2	4	4	3	4	2	5
17	3	5	1	2	1	3	7
18	1	4	2	1	4	6	4
19	5	7	3	2	5	2	2
20	2	6	3	3	6	5	4

Part.#	conf.	intell.	intro.	cont.	anx.	imp.	greg.
1	3	7	6	5	4	4	7
2	6	6	5	2	7	4	5
3	5	7	4	3	1	2	6
4	7	7	4	2	6	5	7
5	5	5	5	3	5	2	7
6	6	7	6	2	4	6	7
7	4	6	3	4	1	3	5
8	4	6	5	2	2	5	6
9	5	7	6	3	3	5	2
10	6	5	5	2	3	4	4
11	7	5	4	5	4	2	5
12	5	7	4	1	5	3	5
13	7	7	3	2	5	6	6
14	6	7	2	3	6	5	5
15	4	6	5	6	2	4	7
16	3	5	6	2	4	6	6
17	6	7	2	1	4	2	7
18	7	6	1	5	3	5	5
19	5	6	2	2	1	3	7
20	6	6	3	3	4	6	7

References

Godden, D. R., & Baddeley, A. D. (1975). Context-dependent memory in two natural environments: On land and under water. *British Journal of Psychology, 66,* 325-331.

Lawton, C. A. (1996). Strategies for indoor wayfinding: The role of orientation. *Journal of Environmental Psychology, 16,* 137-145.

O'Connell, M. A., & Blass, T. (2000, March). *What do cell phones communicate about their owners?* Poster session presented at the annual meeting of the Eastern Psychological Association, Baltimore, MD.

Payne, D. G., & Wenger, M. J. (1998). *Cognitive psychology.* Boston: Houghton Mifflin.

Robinson, K. J., & Roediger, H. L., III. (1997). Associative processes in false recall and false recognition. *Psychological Science, 8,* 231-237.

Sigall, H., & Ostrove, N. (1975). Beautiful but dangerous: Effects of offender attractiveness and nature of the crime on juridic judgment. *Journal of Personality and Social Psychology, 31,* 410-414.